A **HOLIDAY** MAGAZINE

TRAVEL GUIDE

ISRAEL

A HOLIDAY
Magazine

TRAVEL GUIDE

ISRAEL

Prepared with the cooperation of the Editors of HOLIDAY

RANDOM HOUSE *NEW YORK*

Library of Congress Catalog Card Number: 72-140712

ISBN: 0-394-46938-0

Manufactured in the United States of America

CONTENTS

CHAPTER *1*

ISRAEL: LAND AND PEOPLE

When Mark Twain visited Israel about a century ago, he wrote of "forbidding desolation." Sadly, he pictured erosion, malaria-infested swamps, and decomposed terraces. Today, in sharp contrast, there are newly planted trees and square white houses in just-born villages. And there is the vigorous pulse and optimism of a people re-creating soil and nationhood.

It is the mixture of contrasts in practically everything that creates the immediate and unforgettable impression of Israel. Beneath its 8,000 square miles—the size of New Jersey—lie ruins of some of the world's most ancient civilizations: Phoenician, Philistine, Hebrew, Nabatean, Roman, and Greek. Above, a vital, contemporary society is being built. The diversity of the landscape is matched by the people, who come from a hundred different lands.

Israel occupies only a tiny sliver of land, but it has played a large role in human history. Geography cast it as a land bridge between Europe, Asia, and Africa. Throughout history it has been the traditional meeting place between East and West, where the world's faiths, traditions, and cultures have interacted to produce Judaism, Christianity, and Islam.

Its climate is equally diverse. Although it is only 270 miles long and its maximum width is only 70 miles, Israel nevertheless has four climatic regions. To the north lie the gentle green hills of Galilee, with rich soil, plentiful rainfall, and a temperate climate. To the south is the desert known as the Negev with hot days and chilly nights. The coastal plain, with orange groves, resorts, and gleaming white cities, looks like the coast of southern California

Statue of Mordekhai Anilevits at the kibbutz that bears his name

or the French Riviera. A few hours' drive to the east is the hot, almost tropical Jordan Valley. Israel is an irregular strip of land bounded on the north by Lebanon and Syria, on the east by Jordan and Syria, on the southwest by Egypt, and at the southern tip, at the port of Eilat, by the Red Sea. The result is a long frontier of 590 miles of land and 158 miles of water, which has been difficult to defend and is bound to be modified as a result of the Six Day War in June of 1967. Its dominant physical feature is an "S"-shaped range of mountains, running like a spinal column down the center of the country from the Lebanese border to Sinai.

Cutting the mountain backbone are several valleys. The largest is the famous Jezreel (the Greek Esdraelon), which stretches from Haifa to the Jordan Valley, a distance of 30 miles. It is one of the most famous passes in history, a funnel for overland routes leading from Damascus and the Tigris and Euphrates river valleys to Egypt. Saul was slain here by the Philistines; Deborah fought her wars here, and Elijah his contests. It has been coveted for its strategic importance from the time when Israel fought the Canaanites to the present.

Now, the Jezreel is a densely settled green valley, dotted with villages and is known as the bread basket of Israel. It was the first part of the country settled by Israel's modern pioneers. Here they drained the swamps and created new types of villages, the famous *kibbutzim* and *moshavot*. These are like no other farms in the world. In the *kibbutz* all land, equipment, and property is owned by the community. Living standards are the same for everyone, and profits are used to build up the farm. Children not only learn together in schools but live together in their own world. The *moshav* has family-owned farmsteads, but there is an intricate system of mutual aid, cooperative marketing, and purchasing. Both the *kibbutz* and the *moshav* are no longer the bare frontier outposts of early pioneer days. They now have modern mechanized farms and beautiful residential sections and gardens.

The western slopes of the mountains roll gently down to the coastal plain, which borders the Mediterranean for 117 miles. This is the site of the Via Maris, and along it legions of conquerors from Alexander the Great to Napoleon have fought. Long before Alexander, the Phoenicians had fortified cities along this strip of coast, from which they sailed their ships to distant ports.

Today the greatest numbers of Israelis live on this plain. Haifa, Israel's major port, and Tel Aviv, her largest city, are also on this plain. On the coast line are resorts to which Israelis go during the long summer. The two-hour drive from Tel Aviv to Haifa goes through miles of orange, grapefruit, and lemon

Jaffa, twin city of Tel Aviv, as ancient as the other is modern

groves. In the spring the flowers perfume the countryside; in winter the fruit is the country's major export.

It is only an hour's drive from Tel Aviv on this pleasant coast to Beersheba in the harsh desert landscape of the Negev. Beersheba is the legendary city where Abraham first pitched his tents and sunk his wells. Today it is the mushrooming capital of the south and the trading center for nomad Bedouins. The Negev, which means dry lands, occupies 60 per cent of Israel's land surface. Heretofore sparsely inhabited, it is now the focus of a tremendous development drive. Huge conduits bring millions of gallons of irrigation water from the Yarkon River, and a mammoth pipe line is being laid to bring even more water from the Jordan River to this vast desert plain to make possible the growing of many crops on the sandy desert soil. Cotton, ground nuts, sugar beets, and fruit cover thousands of acres.

To the south of the plain, the Negev mountains rise in fantastic shapes. They yield phosphates, clays, and glass sands. At Timna, King Solomon mined his copper, and from Etzion Gever, on the Red Sea, his ships carried it to distant Ophir, returning with cargoes of apes, ivory, peacocks, and gold. Today, Timna is again producing copper, which is shipped from Eilat.

In the northeast shoulder of the Negev is the Dead Sea, the lowest point on the earth's surface, with a salt density so great that one can sit on its water and read a paper. On its shores were the cities of Sodom and Gomorrah, reduced to ashes because of the "lustful abomination" of the citizens, although oil men are now convinced that the destruction was caused by the igniting of a mixture of petroleum and gas. From the dense waters of the Dead Sea, potash, bromides, magnesium, and common salt are extracted.

In contrast to the fierce heat and harsh landscape of the southern desert are the gentle contours and pleasant climate of Galilee in the north. The rich dark soil of its valleys and hillsides are covered with silvery green olive groves and deciduous fruit

Modern harvesters at work in newly fertile fields

orchards bearing the figs, pomegranates, and vines mentioned often in the Bible. Fish ponds dot the countryside and supply the carp served by Jewish families on Friday nights.

Western Galilee is the traditional home of most of Israel's Arab citizens. Their houses, built of local stone, appear to grow out of the hills. However, as everywhere in Israel, there are many signs of change as tradition gives way to progress. Most villages now have electricity and running water, although graceful women balancing water jugs are still seen. Veiled and traditionally garbed women pass others in European dress. Children, instead of working in the fields as in the past, now attend school. Olive trees, sheep, and tobacco are still the bases of village economic life, although in Nazareth, the all-Arab city, industry is developing. But the greatest change involves ownership of land. Eighty per cent of Israeli Arabs now work their own land. They also elect local councils to run village life and send their own representatives to the Knesset, Israel's parliament in Jerusalem.

Nazareth, Capernaum, Tabgha, Mount Tabor, and the River Jordan are among the many places where the Bible story unfolded. In the quiet and serenity of the Galilean hills it is not difficult to visualize this as the land where Jesus grew to manhood and preached to his fellow villagers. The largest single religious site is the Sea of Galilee, shaped like a harp, and therefore called Kinneret in Hebrew. The fishermen of today encounter the same unpredictable storms as did Peter when he sailed this inland lake, and catch the same fish, a notable delicacy when freshly cooked in small lakeshore cafés.

Israelis never tire of proudly relating all the changes they have made in a few years. They discourse about Israel's water resources and its problems. They talk about the rainfall in the north, which amounts to 37.4 inches per year, and they talk about rainfall in the Negev, which is only 1.5 inches a year. They boast of the conduits and pipe lines being built to bring the surplus northern waters down to the parched south where whirling sprinklers spray the water over field and orchard. They proudly tell of the planting of millions of trees on land denuded by goats and sheep. These trees now provide windbreaks, timber, and fruit, and are another weapon in the battle to transform the landscape and make the climate suitable for human habitation.

Israelis have many diverse backgrounds, and there has not been enough time for the development of a national type. The nearest approach are the rough, healthy youngsters who are sometimes brash to the point of arrogance. They are less intro-spective and self-analytical than their parents, who call them "sabras," the name of a cactus fruit, prickly without, sweet within.

Sabras make up less than a third of the total number of Israelis. For the rest, despite many different origins, there are some noticeable common characteristics. They are so voluble that talk-ing seems to be the national sport. Israelis are prepared to discuss all of their and the world's problems, and few seem to doubt that they are less knowledgeable than any cabinet minister. They not only talk, but read and listen. Books and newspapers have a large sale. Variety, concert, and theater tickets are always oversubscribed. The atmosphere is one of youthfulness and a refreshing personal confidence in all that is being built.

Israel's population is about equally divided between those of oriental and occidental origin. Whatever their origin, most have learned to speak Hebrew, either from their children or in adult night schools. Food differences still persist, however. Flat oriental *peeta* or western-type bread, rice or potatoes, lamb or beef, is eaten according to family background. Oriental families produce more offspring, and some still have a patriarchal system of local rule. Religious customs and wedding ceremonies vary, though all adhere to the Jewish faith.

To Israel have come immigrants from North Africa, Asia, and the Middle East. Some had lived as cave dwellers in Tripoli; others in the *mellahs* of Casablanca and other North African cities. Some had been feudal serfs of Arab landlords in mud-hut villages of the Atlas Mountains, while others came with university educations from Baghdad and Cairo.

One very exotic group of immigrants is the entire community of Jews from Travancore on the Malabar Coast of India, where they had lived since the 6th century B.C. Another colorful group are the Yemenites, who, with their traditional skills of working silver and gold, and their exotic dances and music, have added much to the general mosaic of Israel's cultural life. What has brought everyone together, regardless of any differences, is a common need and urge to build a country for themselves. For the children problems of background and custom no longer exist —they are all Israelis, and this is their home.

CHAPTER 2

THE BACKGROUND

There are many ready-made theories "explaining" the character and the problems of the Jewish people and their land but no satisfactory answers as to how a dispersed people survived thousands of years of exile and then returned to the swamps and sands of their ancestral homeland, where they brought themselves and a desolate land to life.

A visit to Israel provides countless impressions, including a very vivid feeling that history for both land and people never stopped—that there was merely a pause lasting 2,000 years.

Until archaeologists discovered the ruins of advanced civilizations in the Jordan Valley, the real antiquity of the Holy Land was not fully known. Jericho, for example, is now regarded as the oldest fortified city known to man, its ramparts built with stone when, at the time, people living in the valley of the Euphrates River were still using mud bricks. Jaffa (Joppa) is now recognized to be the world's most ancient port. Grain was irrigated on the slopes of Israel's mountains long before similar methods were employed in Mesopotamia. Chalcolithic man worked copper at Beersheba at least 500 years before Egypt is known to have mined and used the metal. Twelve skeletons discovered in the caves of Mount Carmel by the British Garrod archaeological expedition in the nineteen thirties established the fact that in the ladder of human evolution the closest species resembling man evolved on this bridge between continents. These skeletons, classified as Homo palestinensis, embody characteristics of both Neanderthal man and Homo sapiens. According to William F. Albright, the celebrated archaeologist, pre-historic man fought

An ancient burial chamber in the catacombs of Beit She'arim

Airview of Massada excavation

and bred in the Jordan Valley as the Ice Age receded. It is hard to believe that this sunny land, now struggling to develop its water resources, was in earliest times a tropical jungle.

Today's Israeli began his history around 2000 B.C. when the patriarch Abraham journeyed from Mesopotamia to the land of Canaan. This was no nomadic invasion but a movement of tribes who had already mastered the irrigation agriculture of the Euphrates, the crafts of Ur, and the caravan routes of the Nile. Many Biblical passages illuminate the background and life of the patriarchs. After Abraham had settled around Beersheba, he linked Mesopotamia and Egypt with caravans. Isaac grew "over a hundred varieties of barley" on the Beersheba plain.

Drought sent Jacob and his sons into Egypt. Joseph's knowledge of agriculture and his consequent relations with the Hyksos rulers, who had spread their dynasty from Mesopotamia to Egypt, made him Pharaoh's prime minister. Enslavement of the Hebrews began on the Nile only when, as the Bible says: "There arose a Pharaoh who knew not Joseph." Historians now accurately pinpoint the date of the Exodus from Egypt as having occurred during the reign of Ramses II in the 13th century B.C., some 250 years before Solomon built his Temple.

Battles with the Canaanites and the Philistines for the country

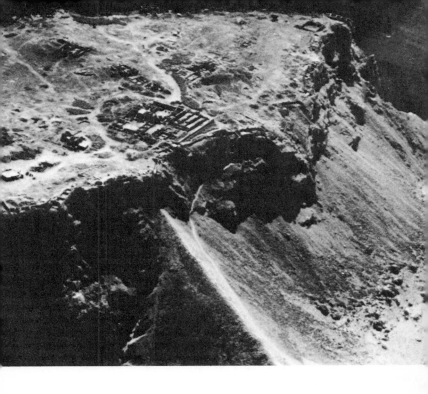

began with Joshua and ended with the conquests of the Judaean monarchy. David won victory over the Edomites and pushed the frontier of his kingdom as far south as Eilat and as far east as the mountains of Edom and Moab. By the 10th century, Solomon had become the copper magnate of the Middle East and, in partnership with neighboring King Hiram of Tyre and the Queen of Sheba, sailed his merchant fleets to Africa and Asia. The Queen of Sheba crossed 1,200 miles of desert with her caravans not only to test Solomon's wisdom and virility but also to test

Mt. Tabor, where Deborah led the Israelites into battle against the Canaanites

his control of the trade routes linking the Red and Mediterranean Seas. Many historians believe that if the business partnership of Solomon and Hiram had resulted in the fusion of both kingdoms, an empire as great as Carthage would have been the result.

For many reasons, such an empire did not arise although the Judaean Kingdom, its capital in Jerusalem, grew wealthy and powerful and became the first great center of monotheism. The Temple built by Solomon as the sanctuary of the one God was noted for its splendor and became the focal point of pilgrimage and prayer for all tribesmen of Israel.

The Judaean Kingdom was conquered by the Babylonians under Nebuchadnezzar in 586 B.C. Thus began the first exile. Many of the princes and great merchants were carried into captivity. The holy Temple of Solomon was destroyed, the fortresses of the Judaean Kingdom were laid in ruins. However, most of the people were allowed to stay, and continued to till their soil and paid an ever growing burden of taxes to the conquerors. The exile continued until the reign of Cyrus, King of Persia from 550? to 529 B.C., who had meanwhile (540-539 B.C.) conquered Babylon. With his permission, the Judaean leaders returned and rebuilt the Temple. A second wave of immigrants arrived from the Persian Empire, led by Ezra and Nehemiah, between 457 and 424 B.C., after the completion of the Second Temple. Although the Judaeans were not permitted to re-establish a sovereign kingdom, liberal Persian rulers allowed them to live as an autonomous people. They were free to practice their religion, and taxes were lightened to enable the people to develop their farms and vineyards and restore their cities. Even after the country was conquered by Alexander the Great in 333 B.C., this autonomy was allowed to continue for a time. However, by 168 Hellenistic rule had become so oppressive that the Judaeans rose in revolt. They were led by a family of priests who, under Judah the Maccabee, established the Hasmonean dynasty that lasted more than a hundred years. This revolt against Greek oppression is remembered by the Jewish people in December of each year in the Hanukkah festival.

Roman domination is traced from 63 B.C., but Hasmonean rule did not end completely until the Roman vassal Herod was placed upon the throne in 37 B.C. The Judaeans rose up in revolt against their Roman masters, and few wars against the Roman Empire were as bloody and heroic as *The Jewish War,* vividly described by the historian Flavius Josephus. Even when the Second Temple was destroyed in 70 A.D. and Jerusalem was captured, the war did not end. Never before in history had a small group of people fought so long, so bitterly, and so well against impossible odds. Guerrilla action grew into mass revolt again in 132 A.D. under the leadership of Simon Bar Kochba. In the three-year struggle that

The crowded Christian Quarter of the Old city of Jerusalem

followed, all Judaea was wrested from Roman hands. Only after the Romans had brought their legions from as far afield as Britain to aid their Middle Eastern armies were the Judaeans finally suppressed.

In the first century of Roman rule, over two million Jews lived in the land of Israel, mostly in Galilee, where in the hilltop town of Nazareth Jesus spent his childhood, and preached in the synagogue of Capernaum on the shores of the Sea of Galilee. In the early days of Byzantine rule, Jews and Christians lived together in common religious communities and fought together against Roman idolatry. During the Byzantine period, which lasted from 395 until 636 A.D., beautiful churches, monasteries, and other religious institutions were built in Jerusalem, in the Negev, and in Galilee.

The last struggle by the Jews to free their land, before the rise of modern Israel, occurred in 614 A.D. when the Persians invaded the land. Historians calculate that at this time, almost six centuries after the Roman conquest, over 200,000 Jews still lived in the country. The battles so exhausted Persians, Byzantines, and Jews that the Arab horsemen of Moab Ibn el Khatab, who swept in from the desert, met with little resistance. The battle of Yarmuk in August 636 A.D. brought the country under Arab rule, and for a thousand years afterwards the land was the scene of foreign and civil wars. Its southern and eastern borders became permanently insecure. Fields were devastated and trees were destroyed. Judaeans and Christians alike were subjected to repeated massacres by raiding Bedouins.

Arab rule in Palestine was finished by the year 1337. As recorded by the Arab historian Ibn Khaldoun: "The realm of the Arabs has been wiped out completely; the power now rests in the hands of non-Arabs, such as the Turks in the east—and the Franks (Europeans) in the north." A succession of caliphates now ruled Palestine, and for hundreds of years there was interdynastic strife. In the midst of these conflicts, the Crusaders first captured the land of Israel in 1099. They finally lost it to the Mameluks in 1291. For a brief time during this era Palestine was a sovereign state.

In 1517 the land came under the rule of the Ottoman Turks. In 13 centuries it had changed hands 14 times. Each time the people made a facile switch of allegiance from one foreign ruler to another. In 1799 Napoleon launched an invasion and his army swept along the famous Via Maris, the coastal route from Egypt. The Turks, with the aid of the British fleet, resisted him at Acre, where he abandoned his campaign. From then until the British took control of the country from the Ottoman Empire during World War I, there were no more invasions. By the end of the 19th century, the mixed population had declined to a mere 150,000 impoverished farmers and townsfolk. The Negev plains had become desolate sand; the valleys of the north had become malaria-infested swamps; the hillsides, denuded by nomadic goats and camels, had become barren. Some 150,000 Bedouins,

Israeli troops in a mock assault landing

seasonally seeking pasture, moved in and out of the land. Of the 150,000 settled inhabitants, 25,000 Jews lived in Jerusalem, Safed, Hebron, and Tiberias. These were descendants of the original Judaeans, who had either remained in the country since Roman times or had returned to die on its holy soil.

Modern Israel, despite popular illusion, was not founded by the establishment of the State on May 14, 1948. Nor was it founded by the British Balfour Declaration in 1917; nor by the Mandate over Palestine, which the League of Nations gave to the British in 1922 on condition that they would facilitate the re-establishment of a Jewish National Home. Modern Israel was founded by pioneer Jews who came from Eastern Europe during the latter part of the 19th century and joined a smaller number of Jews who had remained or had returned before them. These early pioneers settled in marshlands and barren wastes that they purchased from Arab absentee owners.

The earliest of the new Jewish towns and villages were built during the years 1880 to 1922 as was the framework of government and economy inherited by Israel as a state in 1948. The various types of villages; the labor federation, Histadrut; health services and schools; political parties; newspapers—all existed before the United Nations decision, in 1947, to establish Israel as a nation. The actual founding of the State, despite subsequent invasion by Arabs, can be attributed to a pioneer community of 660,000 Jews who by then had established themselves in their ancient homeland.

The 18-year life of Israel as a state is too recent to be called history. It is all immediately apparent. As you walk its streets and talk to its people, you learn of the intake of over one and a half million immigrants in less than 15 years. Nearly everyone is either a survivor of Hitler's Europe or one of the 50,000 Yemenites who trekked across the desert and flew in from Aden during the "Magic Carpet" operation, or one of 125,000 Jews from Iraq; or one of hundreds of thousands who came from North Africa, Eastern Europe, or any one of a hundred other countries.

No country can equal Israel's optimism about the future and the successful outcome of this moving experiment in human relations.

CHAPTER 3

WHAT YOU SHOULD KNOW ABOUT ISRAEL

Since the austerity of the first years, the standard of living in Israel has been rising steadily, to the point that it now rates high on the scale, along with such countries as Holland. Apartments may seem somewhat small by American standards, but are generally no smaller than in Europe. Food is plentiful and cheap.

You will be the subject of disarming hospitality in Israel. Israelis take literally the Biblical injunction to be gracious to the "stranger within thy gates," and so don't be surprised if your guide, taxi driver, or casual acquaintance invites you to his home. If this happens to you, by all means accept, as you will learn much about the country this way.

WHEN TO GO

The pleasantest time to visit Israel is, undoubtedly, in the spring or fall, from March to May and October to November when the days are warm and evenings cool and the country is at its greenest and most attractive. These are also the seasons of traditional holidays and festivals.

But at no time during the year is all the country difficult Although the summer from June to September is warm and virtually rainless, and the coastal plain tends to be humid, it is always possible to make for the cool and dry hilly regions. The

A meeting of the Knesset early in the young country's history

winter season from November to March means lower temperatures and short rainy spells, but even then Tiberias in Galilee and Eilat on the Red Sea provide ideal summer weather for winter vacations. Real cold is very rare anywhere in Israel—snow has been seen just five times in the last seventeen years.

PASSPORTS AND VISAS

You need a visa as well as a valid passport to enter Israel. Actually, however, American and Canadian citizens need not worry about getting the visa as it is granted, without charge, at the point of arrival in Israel. Groups of five to fifty people may obtain a collective visa. An international certificate of vaccination against smallpox is required except in the case of tourists who have been residents for more than fourteen days in a European country, the U.S.A., or Canada immediately prior to arrival in Israel—provided those places are free from smallpox. The vaccination certificate is required, however, for return entry into the United States. Any information can be obtained at the following embassies and consular offices in the United States and Canada.

11 East 70th Street, New York, N. Y. 10021, (212) TR 9-7600

1621 22nd Street, N.W., Washington, D.C. 20008, (202) 483-4100

659 South Highland Avenue, Los Angeles, Calif. 90036, (213) 938-3691

105 Montgomery Street, San Francisco, Calif. 94104, (415) 981-2786

707 Lewis Tower Building, Philadelphia, Pa. 19102, (215) 546-5556

1520 Texas Avenue, Houston, Tex. 77002, (713)225-5417

936 North Michigan Avenue, Chicago, Ill. 60611, (312) 943-0265

805 Peachtree Street, N.E., Atlanta, Ga. 30308, (404) 875-7851

144 Commonwealth Avenue, Boston, Mass. 02116, (617) 266-3800

45 Powell Avenue, Ottawa, Ontario, Canada, (613) CE 2-5305

1555 McGregor Street, Montreal, P.Q., Canada, (514) WE 7-3937

159 Bay Street, Toronto, Ontario, Canada, (416) EM 2-1491

PLANNING YOUR TRIP

To get the most out of your trip, some planning beforehand is essential—and if you are a seasoned traveler, you know that the more information you have about a place before you visit it, the more rewarding your trip. Fortunately there are reams of

Israel's Parliament, the Knesset

material available; advice and information are easy to obtain. The best sources are the Israel Government Tourist Offices, which can help both in planning your trip and getting you around once you arrive. The main offices at this end are in New York at 574 Fifth Avenue, in Chicago at 5 S. Wabash Avenue, in Los Angeles at 615 South Flower Street, and in Montreal, Canada, at 1117 St. Catherine West.

Information and advice are also obtainable at the offices of the El Al Israel Airlines and the Zim Passenger Lines, Ltd. in major American cities, and you will find Government Tourist Information Offices, in over a dozen cities in Israel itself, invaluable sources of information of every sort.

Complementing all this general information, your travel agent will be able to give you the benefit of his experience regarding transportation and reservation arrangements. He will also be able to offer you pre-arranged tours, combining Israel and several other countries, or to Israel alone. Shipping companies, airlines, organizations, and agents all offer such tours, some taking in Israel and various European countries, others concentrating on Mediterranean lands and Israel. For example: Israel, Greece, Italy, Spain; Israel and the Soviet Union; Israel, the Greek Islands and Black Sea; Israel, Italy, France, Switzerland, England.

But one thing is sure: whether you are seeking help planning the trip or on the spot information and advice, you will be met with courtesy by English-speaking people. Israel and the Israelis are interested in promoting tourism to their country and will do their best to make your trip memorable.

HOW TO GET THERE

Most tourists with time to spare combine their visit to Israel with trips to European or Middle Eastern countries. Recognizing this, shipping and airline companies allow for a combined ticket that permits travel there by ship and return by air, or vice-versa, without losing the round trip reduction. Ask your travel agent.

By ship. Several shipping companies run regular schedules to Israel all year round. The Greek Line sails from New York to Haifa, and the following companies operate between European ports and Haifa: Zim Israel Navigation Company, Adriatica, Chandris Cruises, Epirotiki Lines, Hellenic Mediterranean Lines, and Turkish Maritime Lines.

A one-way fare from New York to Haifa by the Greek Line, off season, runs from $360.00 to $451.00 tourist class, and from $543.00 to $888.00 first class. The rates in season are 5 to 10 per cent higher.

By air. Traveling by air presents no problems since Lydda airport is the terminus for fourteen international airlines, most of them operating several flights weekly to Israel from the world's major capitals. El Al and TWA run direct flights from New York. An open round-trip ticket costs $885.60 economy and $1285.60 first class. The same ticket allows for stopovers in European capitals at your leisure.

A big saving can be made from November through March when shipping companies and airlines offer large fare reductions.

One thing to keep in mind, though, if you are planning stopovers before reaching Israel. You can visit Israel directly from the Arab countries by crossing into Israel from Jordan via the Mandelbaum Gate in Jerusalem. Or you may fly from an Arab country to Cyprus and from there to Israel. If you have crossed into Israel via the Mandelbaum Gate, however, the Jordanian authorities will not permit you to recross the frontier.

WHAT TO TAKE

It is a good rule to accent casual informal clothes with a few more dressy things for "occasions," but even then black ties are rarely seen. One story has it that the mayor of Beersheba replied to an Embassy invitation specifying black tie that he guessed he couldn't come since his ties were all colored and his only evening clothes were pajamas. If your trip is in summer, take comfortable, light cottons, sport shirts, slacks or shorts with a sweater or jacket for evenings spent in hilly or desert districts. Good walking shoes and sandals are a must, as are bathing suits and beachwear. Tel

The John F. Kennedy Memorial in the Judean Hills

The modern city of Tel Aviv

Aviv is more dressy than Haifa or Jerusalem, but even there simple cocktail dresses and summer suits are appropriate for hotel dinners and night clubs. Drip-dry clothes are invaluable since laundry and cleaning tend to be expensive and take more time than at home. In spring and fall the warm days are followed by evenings that are quite cool so suits and sweaters are necessary. Winter visitors should remember that rain is short and heavy, and should pack a water-repellent overcoat, overshoes, umbrella, and closed walking shoes. It is worth taking along an extra supply of cosmetics as, although you will find your brands in the shops, prices tend to be higher.

TIPS FOR PHOTOGRAPHERS

Israel is a photogenic country. Bright strong sunshine, clear skies, historic sites, modern projects, and diverse peoples tempt even the most amateur.

Keep your camera and film well protected from heat and dust, and remember that the sunlight is stronger than in the United States or Europe. Black-and-white film may be developed and printed locally, but there are few facilities for processing color or movie film. Bring along a plentiful supply of film, because prices are high. (See below for quantities allowed.)

CUSTOMS

You will find the customs officials courteous and efficient. All reasonable effects and usual travelers' accessories may be brought in. On certain items, however, there are limitations: ½ pint of perfume, 1.33 pints of wine, 1.33 pints of other alcoholic beverages, 24 plates or 10 rolls of film for still cameras, 10 reels of movie film, 250 cigarettes and, while small amounts of coffee are allowed in free, larger ones will be taxed. Gifts up to the value of $40 are duty free, and you can bring gifts up to $100 without an import license though duty will have to be paid. Larger items call for an import license, for which you can apply at any Israel Consulate abroad before departure.

CURRENCY

There is no limit to the amount of foreign currency that may be brought into Israel, and you may also bring in or take out up to 100 Israel pounds in denominations of one and five pounds.

Israeli currency is not difficult to handle. The basic unit is the Israeli pound, which is divided into 100 agorot and each agora into 10 prutot. A point to bear in mind is that the agora is still sometimes called by its old name of "grush" or "piastre."

Coins of one, five, ten, and twenty-five agorot

The rate of exchange, set by the devaluation in November of 1967, is three and one half Israeli pounds to the U.S. dollar; so one Israeli pound is the equivalent of about 28¢. As in all countries, you will get a better rate for your money if you exchange it at an authorized bank or travel agency—rather than when you are paying your bill at a restaurant or shop.

Beware of being stuck with a large block of pounds as departure time draws near. Visitors leaving may reconvert into foreign currency up to the equivalent of $30 (IL 105), and may take out with them IL 100.

You can, of course, take out all items purchased, though their value should not exceed the amount of currency you exchanged officially.

HOW TO GET AROUND IN ISRAEL

The first thing to bear in mind is that Israel is a small country and that places are usually hours apart, never days. There is no difficulty at all in getting around, even to the remotest section, since there is such a wide network of public and private transport available.

By bus. For getting around the cities, buses are the popular means of transport, but, although cheap and frequent, they tend to be crowded and uncomfortable. Taxis are far quicker and more convenient; all of them now have meters, and fares are reasonable. An Israel invention is the "sherut" taxi. They follow the bus routes, pick up passengers at the stops, and charge per seat. It works out slightly more than buses and a lot less than private taxis. They also run between cities.

Travel by inter-urban buses is somewhat more comfortable than in the city buses since standing is limited. Connections can be made to any part of the country, but for truly easeful travel between cities, the "sherut" comes into its own. Roomy seven-seater limousines ply the routes back and forth between the major cities on schedule according to timetable, and take you to your destination quickly for only a little more than you would pay for bus or train fare. There are various companies, mostly cooperatives, running this service, and you can book either through your hotel or at the local office. Most of the drivers, by the way, are shareholders in the company.

By train. Train service between all the main cities is modern, clean, and fast. Rates are low, less expensive than on the buses. From Tel Aviv to Haifa, for instance, a ticket costs about 82¢. Seats may be reserved in advance for a payment of the equivalent of about 8 cents. On all journeys of any length a buffet car is in operation.

By air. Arkia, the Israel Inland Airline, runs daily flights between Tel Aviv, Jerusalem, and Haifa, as well as from these cities to Eliat on the Red Sea and to Rosh Pina in Galilee.

Driving in Israel. Roads between the main cities are generally four lanes, although you shouldn't expect to find the equivalents of American super-highways. All other roads are asphalt paved and of European standard. If you intend to travel on the road to Sodom or in the Galilean hills, make sure that your brakes and steering wheel are in good order. The Israeli public is not very traffic conscious, and so if you're driving, use extra care in populated areas and at night. For some reasons local cyclists, and there are many of them, do not seem to appreciate the value of carrying lights at night.

You drive on the right, as at home, and the road signs are mostly in the form of easily understandable international symbols. Horn blowing within city limits is strictly forbidden.

An International Driver's License as well as national driver's licenses printed in English or French are accepted.

The Automobile Club and Touring Association of Israel provide advice, itineraries, maps, and information at their office at Beit Hadar, 19 Petah Tikva Road, Tel Aviv, telephone 622961. The Israel offices of the A.A.A. are 28 Ahad Ha'am Street, Tel Aviv, telephone 67401

There are plenty of service stations on all the main highways, but they tend to be few and far between on less-traveled roads, so check in advance before setting out. Speed limits in built-up areas are 31 miles per hour (50 km. per hr.), elsewhere 50 (80 km. per hr.). Distances are marked on signposts in kilometers (1 km. equals ⅝ mile). The cost of gasoline is high—about 60¢ a gallon.

Self-drive cars for hire. Cars can be rented at from $5 to $12 per day depending on the type of car. Add to this 8 to 20¢ per kilometer with a minimum daily charge of 100 kilometers.

The three main agencies are:

AVIS RENT-A-CAR:
Tel Aviv: *106 Hayarkon Street, Tel. 444720*

HERTZ RENT-A-CAR:
Jerusalem: *18 King David Street, Tel. 21151*
Tel Aviv: *10 Carlebach Street, Tel. 26414 (Head Office), Hilton Hotel, Tel. 238587*
Haifa: *1 Palmer Street, Tel. 65426*
Lod Airport: *Entrance lobby, Tel. 971165*
Nathanya: *Kikar Ha'atzmaut 8, Tel. 23768*

SIGHTSEEING LTD.:
Tel Aviv: *81 Hayarkon Street, Tel. 56248*
57 Ben Yehuda Street, Tel. 221496
Haifa: *4 Safed Street, Tel. 522727*
5 Nordau Street, Tel. 523666

If your time is limited or if you prefer to relax and be driven around, it is worth considering the tours and excursions that last from half a day to three days and cover all parts of the country. They begin in Jerusalem, Tel Aviv and Haifa. The buses and cabs are spacious and comfortable; the prices are officially approved; and there is the tremendous advantage of having multi-lingual guides who invariably know every nook and cranny of the country and its history.

The Shrine of the Book

If you prefer to hire your own Licensed Guide, the Government Tourist Office or Travel Agency can help you with this.

And finally, you can rent a chauffeur-driven car in any of the three main cities. Several companies rent a manned, air-conditioned car seating 4–6 passengers, at prices ranging from $36 to $42 a day, plus 16¢ per kilometer after the first 200. The driver is a qualified guide.

LANGUAGE

Hebrew is the common spoken language in Israel. Both it and Arabic are official. English, however, is widely understood, certainly in all official or tourist circles. All public notices affecting tourists are printed in English and Hebrew.

Hebrew is an ancient language that has been brought up to date by the adaptation of new words from the old. But apart from official innovations, you may sometimes be startled by the unofficial transpositions from English. The rear axle of a car, for instance, has become "beckexle" while the front axle is "front beckexle."

If you want to practice your French, German, Hungarian, or practically anything else, you will have no difficulty in finding someone to talk to, since most Israelis speak several languages, and the streets can sometimes sound like the Tower of Babel.

HOTELS

To keep pace with the rapid expansion in tourism, hotels are continually being added. In the last year, for instance, both the Sheraton and Hilton chains have built hotels that run close to their American pattern. Hotels are graded by the government into five categories, reflected by stars; the rates are fixed but can vary with the rate of exchange. Five and four star hotels all provide first-class service, are fully air conditioned, most have a private bathroom for each room and, in general, meet the best international standards. Most are clustered in Tel Aviv or its environs, with a fair number in Jerusalem, and the rest in Haifa, Beersheba, Eilat, and other parts of the country, mostly at resorts.

In the heavy tourist seasons of spring or fall it is advisable to book well in advance, or run the risk of being disappointed.

Three star hotels are reasonable and comfortable, but offer fewer amenities. Many have rooms with private showers or baths and air conditioning, but facilities vary considerably from hotel to hotel.

If you are planning a long stay, you may be interested in two and one star establishments which are mostly private family pensions and small hotels. Accommodations generally consist of rooms with hot and cold water; some have private showers, but few boast a lounge or anything except a registration desk and rooms.

Rate ranges for hotels can be found at the beginning of Chapter 7, FACT FINDER.

Numerous Christian hospices provide accommodation with a strikingly low rate for pilgrims, often between three and four dollars per day with full board.

When planning your trip, it is worth bearing in mind that not all small towns have good hotels and some of those in the third category are, frankly, just depressing. But distances in Israel are small enough to enable you to plan your route in such a way that you can almost always finish up your day in a first- or good second-grade hotel.

Motels and hostels are a new feature on Israel roads. To date, only a few have been built, but these are comfortable and clean and generally in extremely interesting surroundings.

If you want to spend one night in a really novel atmosphere, you can't do better than choose a guest house belonging to a kibbutz. These are numerous, set in pleasant country surroundings, provide simple but good food and are scrupulously clean. It will give you a first-hand view of the rural life of Israel and a real chance to meet the people.

For those observing the dietary laws, the Fact Finder indicates whether hotels are kosher or not.

FOOD AND WINES

Israel is not the gourmet's paradise. This does not mean that you will not find the food adequate, well prepared and served, and sometimes fun. It is just that there is no original cuisine of imagination and excitement and few exotic native dishes.

To avoid unpleasantness and "tourist stomach," give your system time to adjust to the hot climate. There are no special bacteria in Israel; but as is true in all Mediterranean countries, they just come in larger quantities due to the heat. If you buy fruit or vegetables, wash them carefully (all Israelis do) and be careful of eating too much of the heavily oiled oriental food until you are acclimatized.

A list of recommended restaurants is available from the Government Tourist Office. The blue-and-gold badge that these places display means that hygiene conditions have been approved.

In the luxury hotels the menus carry elegant names and meals are beautifully served, but the food is pretty much the standard hotel food you find anywhere. Outside hotels you can choose between oriental and European cooking. The quality varies, of course. Most restaurants offer staple European fare, and many feature traditional Jewish cooking, chicken soup with kneidlach,

Cabbage farming on a kibbutz

gefilte fish, carp and other items familiar to Jewish menus the world over.

Oriental cooking is popular with the native-born Israeli and, of course, those hailing from North Africa. Tourists with culinary curiosity should sample these favorite Middle Eastern dishes.

Peeta—the flat, pancake-shaped bread seen all over the Orient. It splits in the middle and is served with all manner of things, as a sort of sandwich.

Felafel—served in kiosks everywhere, it is the Israeli hot dog. Made of heavily spiced small balls of ground chick peas, deep fried, smothered with vegetables and stuffed into peeta.

Taheena—an appetizer paste of ground sesame seeds, oil, and garlic, scooped up with pieces of peeta.

Humus—similar to taheena, but this time made with ground chick peas.

Lamb is, of course, the staple meat of the oriental cuisine, and *shashlik* and *kebab* are popular as are vegetables stuffed with rice, meat, and tomatoes, called *machshi*.

Israelis themselves are great people for vegetables and dairy foods. All local products, they are excellent as is the wide variety of cheeses now being made. The local yogurt-like *leben* and *lebenia* are both worth sampling, and so are the superb fruits, especially the melons, oranges, grapefruit, mandarins, grapes, and pomegranates when in season. You may find the salads disappointing in summer, as the sun is too hot for growing leafy vegetables and storage facilities are limited. Be sure to try the Israeli breakfast, which includes a variety of pickled herrings, fresh vegetables, olives, and cheeses instead of your usual eggs and cereal.

When in the area, remember to visit the sea and lake shore cafés of Akko, Tiberias, and Jaffa, where fish are caught on the doorstep, fried, and brought to the table. Fish in general is good, but limited in variety, although the exotic types caught in the Red Sea have by now acquired a measure of reknown.

Israel cafés deserve some attention, not so much for their

culinary achievements, as for the local color and interest they provide. Most people have their favorite spots, and here, for the price of a cup of coffee, they may sit for hours, meet friends, deal with their mail, play chess, and often have their postal address. The Tel Aviv sea front abounds in these, mostly with tables outside where you can watch the crowds mill by.

A footnote warning for the American coffee fiends. If you are an expert, you may prefer to pass up the coffee entirely and drink tea instead. The art of making good coffee is not unknown to the Israeli, but the finest coffees are imported and for many prohibitively expensive.

You will find that everybody drinks bottled orange or grapefruit juice, *mitz*, partly because it is extremely good and partly because the water, although pure, is not too good in taste. Vast quantities of bottled soda water, *gazoz*, are also consumed.

There is a wide range of local beers, brandies, and table wines. They vary considerably in quality, and your best bet is to ask the advice of your waiter. Whisky is not produced locally and imported brands are subject to heavy tax, which makes them expensive.

TIPPING

Israel is one of the few countries without an embarrassing tipping problem. In all hotels and most restaurants the service charge makes tipping unnecessary, unless, of course, you have received special services that you feel merit the extra.

If you use a "sherut" taxi, you are not expected to tip, and Israelis never tip the regular taxi driver. He is often a share-holder in his taxi cooperative, and is, in any case, relatively well paid, and often too proud to accept tips. With a hired private guide or driver, there is no hard and fast rule; the amount you give him is entirely up to you. But don't be too surprised if your tips are refused sometimes. Many Israelis have a strongly defined antipathy towards tipping.

SHOPPING

The combination of its geographical position and the fact that its inhabitants come from many lands bringing with them many different skills, makes shopping for gifts a wonderful experience here. If you prefer reliable courteous service, then go to the shops recommended in the Ministry of Tourism Shopping Guide and recognizable by the official emblem displayed. But if you enjoy getting off the beaten track and are confident of your bargaining prowess, get to the smaller shops off the main streets and into the markets.

Wherever you go, look for the beautiful Yemenite embroidered blouses and accessories and their delicately wrought jewelry. Another of the best buys in Israel is in copper and brass articles sold in many shops. They range from antique to ultra–modern. You must beware, however, of getting stuck with older pieces on which new work has been imposed. In fact, if you are searching for genuine antiques in glass, metal, or coins, you will be well advised to look in the established shops even if prices are higher.

Newer but very attractive are the olive wood chess sets, necklaces, candlesticks, and dishes. Traditional Persian carpets are also a good buy as are the bright hard-wearing rugs made by immigrant weavers from North Africa. There is a wide selection of ceramics, some beautiful in design and color, some primitive.

You will have to use sign language for your bargaining in Jaffa's flea market, but you will find silver and gold filigree jewelry sold by weight, and some of the green-looking junk you can pick up may eventually turn out to be unusual copper ornaments when polished. Nearby, the centuries-old town of Jaffa has been turned into an entrancing art and entertainment center. The picturesque houses have been converted into studios and galleries, where contemporary art and handicrafts are sold at night as well as during the day.

If you are visiting the Druze villages on the Carmel, look at the hand-woven straw baskets, trays, dishes, and bags, which make unusual and, moreover, lightweight gifts. For the musical, the skin drums found in Nazareth and Akko are interesting and the artistic should head for Ein Hod and Safed, the artists' villages where original paintings, sculpture, pottery, and jewelry can be found.

Manufactured goods tend to be expensive in Israel, but there are some notable exceptions that make worth-while buys. Jersey suits, blouses, and sweaters are smart, extremely well made and not too expensive. Furs are also relatively cheap.

Men's suits of fine imported wool or gabardine are well tailored and far cheaper than in the United States. The prices range from $65 to $85 and they can be ready within 48 hours, but remember, it is only common sense to order at least a week before you plan to leave. Handmade shoes are cheaper than in any Western country.

A husband and wife from Yemen pursue their ancient craft in Tel Aviv

Worth visiting is any of the *Maskit* stores, which runs a cottage industry enterprise giving women in new settlements an opportunity to use their native handwork. They have a first-class designer and are making beautiful clothes. *Wizo* gift shops are also an outlet for the handwork of newcomers, and specialize in embroidered clothes.

Israel sizes correspond to those of Europe:

MEN'S SHIRTS :	*American*	14½	15	15½	16	16½	17
	Local	37	38	39	41	42	43
TROUSERS AND JACKETS :	*American*	36	38	40	42		
	Local	46	48	50	52		
LADIES' DRESSES:	*American*	10	12	14	16	18	20
	Local	36	38	40	42	44	46
SWEATERS AND BLOUSES :	*American*	34	36	38	40	42	44
	Local	40	42	44	46	48	50

Duty-free shops at Lod airport and leading hotels sell foreign perfume, liquor, cameras, and watches against payment in foreign currency. They are sent to your point of departure for pickup.

SPORTS AND DIVERSIONS

Although Israelis are sports enthusiasts, facilities are still somewhat limited. The long summer and superb Mediterranean beaches make the country ideal for swimming, surf riding and sailing, although one should be careful of the strong undercurrents in some spots. Eilat provides all-year-round conditions for bathing and water sports especially for the newly popular scuba diving. Caesarea, on the coast between Tel Aviv and Haifa, is also popular for skindiving and snorkeling because of the interesting underwater ruins to be explored. Fishing tackle is readily obtainable, and the coastal waters and rivers provide good fishing. Fresh-water bathing in the Sea of Galilee is pleasant, and there are public swimming pools in the cities, in rural settlements and in many hotels.

Soccer is the great national game and international matches are held frequently in the Ramat Gan Stadium outside Tel Aviv. Tennis and basketball are favorites and courts are available in the cities and many smaller towns. The one and only golf course in Israel is to be found at Caesarea.

There is a wealth of cultural and artistic activity going on most of the time. The Israel Philharmonic holds regular concerts in each of the three main cities, often performing under distinguished guest conductors or with world famous soloists. Every Tuesday evening in Jerusalem the Israel Radio Orchestra performs, and there are numerous chamber music groups, local orchestras and choral societies. The Israel National Opera is housed in Tel Aviv

Zeev Yaskiel, young Israeli artist at the colony of Ein Hod

as are some fine theaters. These, however, perform in Hebrew, although many of the plays are translations from familiar foreign ones and an English synopsis is generally provided.

Showings of classical and contemporary art abound both in the museums and galleries of the main cities and in the museums of the smaller towns and rural settlements. Many have interesting collections that include antiquities and local archaeological finds. The most famous are discussed in the following chapters.

A particularly successful attempt to develop the native talents that immigrants brought to the country can be seen in the Inbal dance group. These Yemenite dancers, who have toured the world's capitals with outstanding success, perform regularly in the three main cities.

Movie houses show a wide selection of films from practically every country, but remember that tickets are purchased for specific performances. Movie-going in Israel for the tourist is a new experience because no matter what the language of the original, there are always sub-titles in English, French, and Hebrew, so many in fact that they often take up a large part of the screen and are frequently in themselves amusing.

For the late-nighters there is entertainment to be found in the night clubs and the cabarets of the leading hotels and some restaurants. But this is on a small scale and it is not Israel's strongest point, although performers can often be quite good. The small satirical clubs are far better, but the language used is Hebrew. Night life is mostly concentrated in the Tel Aviv, Jaffa, Ramat Gan area, but some of the small bars and cafés in other parts of the country often have some sort of entertainment.

A few special events during the year should be noted: The Israel Festival of Music and Drama. The week-long Music Festival at Kibbutz Ein Gev on the Sea of Galilee during Passover is worth visiting both for the quality of the performances and for the natural beauty of the setting.

The Druze "Fantasia" on the occasion of the feast of Nebi Shueib identified with Jethro (Moses' father-in-law).

The folk-dance festival at Kibbutz Dalia in the Hills of Ephraim during the summer, which brings together dancers from all parts of the country.

Meandering alleys and streets of the Old City of Jerusalem

Finally, if you are interested in meeting and visiting Israelis in their homes, mention this at any Government Tourist Information Office and you will receive an invitation. There are many who are eager to extend hospitality to you, and their names are listed at the office. You may even choose members of your own profession or people with whom you share common interests and hobbies, but in any case, it will give you the opportunity to get to know some Israelis more intimately.

ISRAEL'S HOLIDAYS

Jewish holidays are celebrated according to the Hebrew calendar and the corresponding English dates each year can be supplied by the Government Tourist Office. All holidays begin on the preceding evening, and in many cases this is really when the festivities take place.

Tu B'Shvat (15th Shvat), January, New Year of the Trees, when children all over the country plant saplings.

Purim (14th Adar), March, the most joyous of the Jewish holidays, recalling the deliverance of the Jews by Queen Esther from Haman. Highlight is the "Adloyada" or carnival parades in all the main cities with decorated floats attended by thousands of children in costume. It is the season for balls, masquerades, and parties, both public and private. One of the most noted is the ball at Ein Hod, the artists' colony near Haifa.

Pesach (Passover) (15th-22nd Nissan), April, commemorating the Exodus from Egypt. All hotels hold a Seder for visitors and they are also welcomed by kibbutzim holding their communal Seder. It is the time of the first traditional pilgrimage to Jerusalem.

Yom Ha'atzmaut (Independence Day) (5th Iyar), May, Israel's big national holiday celebrating the birth of the State. The entire population turns out to dance and sing in the street on the preceding evening. Parades and pageants take place throughout the country.

Lag B'Omer (18th Iyar), May, marks the end of 33 days of mourning for the persecution of Jews and is joyfully celebrated with bonfires and dancing. Highlight is the Hassidic pilgrimage to the cenotaph of Rabbi Shimon Bar Yohai in Meron, where they dance and sing throughout the night.

Shavuot (6th Sivan), June, Festival of the First Fruits and the Giving of the Law on Mount Sinai. Harvest festivals take place all over the country with colorful ceremonies of children bearing the first fruits. Second of the traditional pilgrimages to Jerusalem.

Rosh Hashana (1st and 2nd Tishri), September, Jewish New Year ushering in Ten Days of Penitence. Services are held in all synagogues.

Yom Kippur (10th Tishri), September or October, Day of Atonement. It is the most solemn day of the Jewish year, of fasting and prayer. It begins with the traditional Kol Nidrei prayer in the synagogue on the previous evening.

Sukkot (15th-22nd Tishri), September or October Feast of Tabernacles. On balconies and in courtyards families erect the bedecked Tabernacle (Sukkah) in which they eat and pray. Third of the traditional pilgrimages to Jerusalem, with ceremonies held on Mount Zion.

Simhat Torah (22nd Tishri), October, Day of the Rejoicing in the Law. Singing and dancing in all the synagogues and in the streets, particularly in the Hassidic and oriental districts in Jerusalem.

Hanukkah (25th Kislev-2nd Tevet), December, Feast of Lights, in commemoration of the Maccabean victory over the Syrian Greeks. Lights are kindled in public places and houses all over Israel, and the traditional eight-branched *menorah* is seen everywhere. A chain of runners bears lighted torches from Modi'in, the birthplace of the Maccabean rebellion, to Mount Zion in Jerusalem.

Christian holidays. Christian ceremonies take on a special significance in Israel when Holy Days are celebrated on the very sites where the events occurred. The following is a list of the places where special ceremonies are held.

GOOD FRIDAY in Jerusalem

EASTER in Jerusalem

PENTECOST in Jerusalem

CHRISTMAS in Bethlehem and Nazareth

FEAST OF THE ANNUNCIATION in Nazareth

FEAST OF ST. JOHN THE BAPTIST at Ein Kerem

FEAST OF THE VISITATION at Ein Kerem

FEAST OF THE PROPHET ELIAS on Mount Carmel, Hafia

FEAST OF THE TRANSFIGURATION on Mount Tabor.

FEAST OF THE ASSUMPTION in Jerusalem

THE SABBATH

Sabbath begins at sunset on Friday and ends at sunset on Saturday. During this period all Government offices, shops, and places of entertainment are closed, except for emergency pharmacies and a few restaurants and cafés that remain open. All public transport ceases, with the exception of some bus services in Haifa, but "sherut" taxis do operate along the main bus lines in Jerusalem and Tel Aviv.

Although you may drive your car, it is good form as well as

A yearly procession to Mt. Zion in Jerusalem

wise not to drive through orthodox sections of town or city. If you need gas, remember to fill up before the Sabbath comes in. There may be a sign in your hotel dining room asking you not to smoke there on Friday or Saturday; on the other hand, if ashtrays are on the table, you are free to do as you wish. On Saturday evening everything comes to life again, including transportation and entertainment, and the streets are thronged for this is Israel's night out. Sunday is a normal working day.

SOME USEFUL FACTS

Postal system. The postal system is like those of most Western countries. Main and branch offices may be identified by a bright blue sign bearing a leaping deer in white. They are closed on Saturdays. Air mail is delivered to all parts of the world, and rates vary according to the nature and weight of the article.

Telegraph and telephone. Central telegraph offices are open night and day including Saturday. At regular hours telegrams may be sent from any branch post office. Telegrams may also be sent by phone. Public telephones in post offices or street booths require a token or two ten-agorot coins. Long-distance calls should be booked at your hotel or at a post office. The local telephone directory is published both in Hebrew and English, so you should have no trouble in locating your number.

Hours. Israel is a country of the early start and midday siesta, so plan your shopping or trips to the bank accordingly. In fact, it would be just as well to use the midday for rest as this is when the sun is hottest.

Banks are open to the public from 8:30 A.M. to 12:30 P.M. and 4 to 5 P.M. They close at 12 noon on Friday and days preceding holidays. Shops are generally open from 8 A.M. to 1 P.M. and 3:30 to 7 P.M. They, too, close at noon on Friday and days preceding holidays. Government offices receive the public from 9:30 A.M. to 12 noon in summer, and in winter until 4 P.M. On Friday this changes from 7:30 A.M. to 1 P.M.

Government Tourist Information Offices are generally open from 8 A.M. to 7 P.M. except on Friday when they close at 3 P.M.

Israel is two hours ahead of Greenwich Time and seven hours ahead of Eastern Standard Time. When it is noon in New York and 5 P.M. in London, it is 7 P.M. in Tel Aviv.

Newspapers and magazines. European editions of the New York *Times* and *Herald Tribune* take a day or two to reach the central newsstands and main hotels. *Life* and *Time* and other American periodicals are also available.

To keep up with the news there is one good daily paper in English, the *Jerusalem Post,* which, apart from covering local affairs, gives a fairly wide world coverage. English books are plentiful and the Israel Broadcasting Service carries several English news broadcasts each day.

There are 18 daily and 2 afternoon newspapers in a variety of languages. Out of the 300 odd periodicals published locally, 200 are in Hebrew while the rest are in a multitude of languages including English.

Emergencies. Medical and dental attention is easily obtainable even in small towns. Professional standards are high, fees moderate, and most doctors speak several languages including English.

First aid and emergency treatment is available day and night from the Magen David Adom (equivalent to the Red Cross). Israel hospitals are included in the American Blue Cross.

Electric current. If you are bringing electrical appliances, remember that Israel's electric current is AC 220 volts, single phase, 50 cycles. The European type plug—2 round prongs—is used in Israel. Get a conversion plug for your electric razor. Your dealer or electrician can give you further advice.

Tobacco. English and American cigarettes are obtainable at all hotels and street kiosks but are expensive, selling at more than double U.S. prices. Local Virginia cigarettes sell for about half as much with popular oriental and blended brands much cheaper.

Weights and measures. Israel weights and measures use the metric system as follows:

1 METER = 3.28 feet or roughly 1 yard
1 KILOMETER = 0.62 mile or roughly ⅝ mile
1 KILOGRAM = 2.2 lbs.
1 LITER = 1.76 pints

A quick way to convert kilometers into miles is to divide by 8 and multiply by 5.

Useful addresses. While most Embassies, including the United States, are in Tel Aviv, all have Consulates in Jerusalem and Haifa.

Shipping packages. There are no restrictions on the number of parcels a visitor may send out of Israel. Packages should be clearly marked with the words "Gift Enclosed" on the outside, and it is advisable to have them insured.

CHAPTER 4

JERUSALEM

For thousands of years men have talked of "going to Jerusalem." They were not thinking of the rugged Judaean hills that command the approaches to the city but rather of the eternal aspirations of man that it symbolized. It is for all that, no less a "going up" in the terrestial sense as the last part of the 44-mile road from Tel Aviv winds ever upwards along the side of rose-tinted rock until the traveler feels he is about to leave earth for heaven. The speed at which most drivers take the curves and drops does nothing to allay the feeling, but you can relax because you always get there. Suddenly on a plateau at the very top rise the stone-faced buildings and red-tiled roofs of the capital.

Even today, amid the lively chatter of the streets and the modern architecture around, you cannot but be aware that this is Jerusalem, the oldest city in human history, dating back to remotest antiquity and sacred to Christendom, Islam, and Judaism.

At the time of Abraham, it was already a city known by the Amorites as Shalem. "Yerra" in their tongue meant "foundation of" and "Shalem" was a god of their pantheon. Little change was needed for the Hebrews to transform this to "Yerushalayim," meaning City of Peace.

It was Solomon the Wise, the son of David, who made Jerusalem the religious and spiritual center for the tribes of Israel when he built his magnificent Temple there. After the division of the kingdom, it remained the capital of Judah until 586 B.C. when the Babylonian king Nebuchadnezzar razed the city and Temple to the ground. His was the first of a succession of conquests by invading powers. For over 2,500 years Jerusalem

The Western Wall, Old Jerusalem

Rachel's Tomb in Jerusalem

changed hands many times, suffering under continuous outside domination except for short intervals when local uprisings achieved Jewish independence and Jerusalem again became the capital. Greeks, Romans, Byzantines, Arabs, Crusaders, and Turks all fought for its possession, but all that remains of the empires are a host of ruined buildings and archaeological fragments.

From time to time, as foundations for new homes are blasted, a burial cave, a section of an aqueduct or ancient cistern are revealed, and the area is roped off by the Department of Antiquities. The greatest excitement is when the discovery is Judaean in period, an understandable prejudice among a populace so interested in rediscovering its severed past.

The last of the foreign rulers were the British, who, in 1917, captured the city from the Turks and occupied it. During the Israel War of Independence of 1948, the Old City, where many of the important relics and sites sacred to the three religions are located, fell into Jordanian hands. The New City, which had grown from Jewish suburbs around the old walls, was held by the Israeli Army despite fierce attack and siege, and this was declared Israel's capital. After the Six Day War in June 1967 the two parts of Jerusalem were re-united as Israeli territory.

Local patriotism abounds in Israel, but there is no disputing the claim of the Jerusalemite that his is the center of government and learning. If nothing else, its geography sets it slightly apart

The Shrine of the Book, Jerusalem

from the rest of the country. Remembering how Jerusalem was besieged in 1948, suburban housing estates now ring the city boundaries, agricultural settlements guard the peaks surrounding it, and new roads have been hewn through the mountains, linking it with the coast.

There is such a wealth of historic association with Jerusalem that it is indeed difficult to know where to start—but a quick look around the center of the city will help you get your bearings. Fortunately, a law enforcing the use of stone for building in the city has prevented it from acquiring the bleak, white concrete appearance of much of the suburban housing in Israel. But the city's dignified and historic aura acts as a strangely contrasting background to the effervescence of its polyglot population, a large percentage of whom are immigrants of recent years. To see it most clearly, you should wander through the three main streets that form the heart of the city—Jaffa Road, Ben Yehuda Street, and King George Avenue. Although not particularly elegant, there are around them some places well worth visiting.

The Old City. The city within the walls contains some of the holiest sanctuaries of Christianity, Judaism and Islam. The sacred exists side by side with the pagan, the latter manifesting itself especially in the colorful bazaar, which extends through several miles of sometimes covered alleys, streets and stairs. Off the main arteries are charming, quiet quarters, often within their own walls, belonging to the various communities. Typical of these are the Latin, Greek and Armenian Patriarchates. A walk through these compounds will turn up no end of surprises in little piazzas and cloisters, exotic oriental churches and chapels, crusader remnants and similar delightful discoveries. *The Western Wall,* also known as *Wailing Wall,* is the holiest of Jewish sites, the only remnant of the walls surrounding the Temple of Biblical times. The adjoining *Jewish Quarter* was largely destroyed during the War of Independence and the ensuing 20 years of Jordanian control, but some of the synagogues and *yeshivot* are being reconstructed. The most important Christian holy site is the *Church of the Holy Sepulchre,* which stands on Golgotha, the traditional site of the crucifixion, burial and resurrection of Jesus. To the church, starting near *St. Stephen's Gate,* leads the *Via Dolorosa,* the way taken by Jesus from the place where he was condemned to Golgotha. Along the way are 14 stations where he halted. Every Friday at 3 p.m. a pilgrims' procession retraces the steps of Jesus. The *Dome of the Rock* marks the spot whence Mohammed is said to have ascended to heaven, and is the third most important Moslem site after Mecca and Medina. It is easily the most resplendent building in Jerusalem, dominating the Temple area and sheltering the rock where Abraham prepared to sacrifice Isaac.

The area outside the old city also has a large concentration of holy sites. The *Garden Tomb* is considered by certain Christian authorities to be the burial place of Jesus. The *Mount of Olives* is associated with the ascension of Jesus. From ancient times up to the present, the mountain has served as a Jewish cemetery, based on the belief that the Messiah will enter Jerusalem from here, coinciding with the resurrection of the dead. At the foot of the mountain, where the *Kidron Brook* continues

The Dome of the Rock, Old Jerusalem

through the *Valley of Jehoshafat* (Kidron Valley), are a number of ancient tombs whose interesting shapes, displaying Hellenistic elements, have been carved out of the mountain side. These are the *Pillar of Absalom,* the *Tombs of the Hezir Family* and of *Zechariah.* Slightly to the east of the mountain's summit are *Bethpage* and *Bethany,* places mentioned in the gospels. The latter was the home of Lazarus, whom Jesus raised from the dead. At the foot of Mount of Olives is *Gethsemane,* where Jesus retired with his disciples before his arrest. The slope of the mountain is here covered with ancient olive trees, which explains the Hebrew origin of the name, meaning olive press. There are two important churches here, the Russian *Church of Mary Magdalene,* and the *Church of All Nations* (Basilica of the Agony). Nearby is the *Tomb of the Virgin.* Across the Valley of Jehoshafat is the *Pool of Shiloah* and the 1700 foot long water tunnel constructed by King Hezekiah in 700 B.C. in order to bring water into the city's walls during siege.

The continuation of the Mount of Olives to the North is called *Mount Scopus.* In 1925 the Hebrew University was established here, with the construction of a number of imposing buildings, including the *Hadassah Hospital* which is linked to the Medical School of the University. In 1948 the compound had to be abandoned as a result of hostilities, and the university and Hadassah hospital built new quarters in other parts of the city. Now that the area is once again freely accessible, the buildings, which have suffered from neglect and fighting during the past 19 years, will be repaired and reactivated. The university amphitheater offers a superb view of the Dead Sea and the desert of Judaea. Also on Mount Scopus is a *British War Cemetery* for soldiers who fell in the area during the World Wars.

Mount Zion is partly outside the city walls. Going up it, you enter an area that was part of Biblical Jerusalem, and archaeological excavations have already uncovered here sections of the Upper City of the 5th century B.C. It is little wonder that this is a hill sacred to Judaism and Christianity, and is the scene of pilgrimage and prayer throughout the year. Climbing the hill, you pass the *Valley of Hinnom,* in ancient times known as Gehenna, the Valley of Depravity and Sin. Steps lead up to the summit of the hill to the *Abbey of the Dormition* where, according to Christian tradition, the Virgin Mary fell into her eternal sleep.

To the left, through a medieval courtyard is the *tomb* that is said to hold the remains of King David. The upper story of the building is sacred to Christians, who call it the *Coenaculum* and believe that here Jesus and his disciples celebrated the first night of Passover and partook of the famed Last Supper.

Leaving the old city behind, you seem to enter a different

The National Museum, Jerusalem

world, of wide, tree-lined streets, green parks and modern buildings. Also in the new city the use of the local limestone is mandatory for building, which gives Jerusalem its special character. On King David Street the tower-topped YMCA building is one of the most elaborate of the institution's branches in many countries. On King George Street are a number of public institutions, such as *Heichal Shlomo* (Supreme Religious Center), the *Sochnut* (Jewish Agency) and the *Yeshurun Synagogue,* one of the best known in Jerusalem.

Mea She'arim. On the other side of Jaffa Road you will find one of the most colorful sections of the city—the old orthodox quarter of Mea She'arim. In striking contrast to the modernity of the rest of Israel, here you find the cobbled streets crowded with stalls and twisted lanes with their dingy shops and shuttered houses. It is the home of the pious who have brought with them the traditions of Eastern Europe, and the garb of the Middle Ages, including the long black kaftans and fur hats. Even the young boys who spend most of the day studying the Torah (the Law) wear side locks and dress much as their elders. The community is made up of a myriad of sects, each with its own revered leader and synagogue, and the tour on Friday evening of these synagogues can be one of the unforgettable experiences of your visit to Jerusalem. By sundown, on that day, traffic to

and from the quarter has ceased, the gates leading into it have been closed, and to the shrill note of the *shofar* (ram's horn) the Sabbath has been introduced.

Not far away from the Mea She'arim is the Bukharian quarter populated by Jews from Southern Russia. They are an interesting people whose colorful traditional costume and distinctive, ornamented synagogues are unceasing subjects for the photographer.

Further north, through the district known as Beit Israel is one of the most beautiful areas in the city, known as *Sanhedriyah*. In the delightful public gardens, situated on high ground, are the tombs of the members of the Sanhedrin, the Supreme Court of Israel in Biblical times. According to tradition, the Court's 71 members were always buried in these caves, called by Christians "The Tombs of the Judges."

Biblical Zoo. On the way back to the city be sure to stop at the Biblical Zoo, for it is unique. Housed here are all the animals, birds, and reptiles mentioned in the Scriptures, surrounded by the appropriate trees and plants. Each cage bears an inscription of the Biblical passage where mention of the animal appears. One of the most coveted treasures is the Syrian bear family, almost half of the species surviving today. The children of Jerusalem swarm over this beautiful setting, from kindergarten tots to any and every age.

Russian Compound. Back on Jaffa Road, approaching the Jaffa Gate and the Old City, you will find on your left a large complex of buildings surrounded by a wall, grouped around a beautiful cathedral whose green dome is topped with a gold cross. This is the Russian Compound originally built by the Russian Orthodox Church to house its faithful on their pilgrimages to Jerusalem. In front of the cathedral, behind a railing, is an enormous stone column almost 40 feet long which is thought by archaeologists to have been quarried for Herod's Temple, but abandoned when it was accidentally broken.

After the Russian Revolution the number of pilgrims understandably dropped off considerably, and although the compound still belongs to the church, a number of the buildings are used by the government. Here you will find the central police headquarters and the building in which the Supreme Court sits.

In the years that Jerusalem was divided, the administrative and cultural center of the city moved westward. This area, with its modern buildings and pleasing landscaping, is full of interest for the visitor.

The Israel Museum. This remarkable complex of buildings, set between the Hebrew University and the Monastery of the Cross, includes a series of museums notable for their architecture as well as the fine collections they contain: *The Samuel Bronfman Museum of Archaeology,* which spans the history and cultures of the land of the Bible from pre-history to the 17th century; *The Bezalel National Art Museum* with its exhibitions of classic and modern art and fine collections of Jewish ceremonial objects; *The Billy Rose Art Garden,* designed by Isamu Noguchi and containing collections of modern sculpture by Moore, Lipschitz, Epstein, and other greats; and *The Shrine of the Book* displaying the famous Qumran (Dead Sea) Scrolls, the Bar Kochba Letters, and other ancient documents. The museum also operates the well-known *Rockefeller Museum* in the Old City, with its comprehensive collection from excavations in Palestine.

In nearby *Rehavia,* a charming residential section several blocks south, is the home of President Zalman Shazar, notable for its disarming modesty and entirely in keeping with the character of its occupant. In this area, workmen digging the foundations of a new house, recently came upon the *Alfasi cave.* Probably dating from the 2nd century B.C., it consists of a rock-cut passage and chambers containing burial niches with walls decorated by various drawings.

Government Center. Here, among the Judaean Hills, the Government Center called the Kirya is rising. The first buildings to go up were the *Treasury, Ministry of Interior,* and *Prime Minister's Office.* On the highest point in the area stands the new building of Israel's *Knesset* (Parliament). The interior has been enriched by creations of contemporary Israel artists and by mosaics and Gobelins by Marc Chagall. The entrance gates are the last work of the late sculptor David Palombo. The building can be visited when the Knesset is not in session. Other ministries are planned. In the Kirya garden a *6th-century Christian mosaic,* forming the bed of a water pool, and a replica of the American Liberty Bell, a gift of the city of Philadelphia, are worth your attention.

Hebrew University. On the hills facing the Kirya and overlooking the Valley and Monastery of the Cross is the magnificent new Hebrew University campus on the heights of Givat Ram. It has already acquired fame as one of the most beautiful of modern universities, with contemporary but highly diversified architecture. The vestibule floor of the *Administration Building* at the entrance is adorned with a 5th-century mosaic. In the center of the campus is the *National and University Library,* which houses one of the world's great collections of books and priceless manuscripts, and at the southern end is the unusual synagogue distinctive for its egg-shaped white cupola.

When Israel's new rocket was launched, many people asked why it was called *shavit,* and the answer was that this is an ancient word for a meteor. This is but one of the functions of the *Language Academy* on the university campus: to meet contemporary needs with words from an ancient tongue. And when you decide to change your name, as do many immigrants, the Academy is there to offer suggestions of a Hebrew equivalent of your old name or a brand new one to start your new life.

Beyond the University, Herzl Road leads you to *Mount Herzl,* where you will find the simple tomb of the founder of modern Zionism and the military cemetery. Nearby is *Memorial Hill* with archives honoring and recording the fate of six million Jews murdered by the Nazis in Europe.

From Mount Herzl the road winds down into a pleasant valley of orchards and vineyards. On this hillside is located the village of *Ein Kerem,* where St. John the Baptist was born. A number of Christian churches and monasteries have been built here in his memory. Among them is the Church of the Visitation, the lower story of which contains an ancient cistern called Mary's Well and an alcove that concealed John from the Roman soldiers.

Recently opened at Ein Kerem, and built on a conspicuous height, is the *Hadassah-Hebrew University Medical Center,* the largest and most up-to-date hospital in the entire Middle East. Be sure to visit its synagogue with the twelve stained-glass windows created by Marc Chagall, one window for each of the twelve tribes of Israel.

CHAPTER 5

TOURS FROM JERUSALEM

If Jerusalem itself is full of "musts," the surroundings of the city are no less interesting. Most of the sites described below are included in half-day tours from Jerusalem.

RACHEL'S TOMB—BETHLEHEM—HEBRON

From the railway station, Hebron Road runs southwards past immigrants' housing projects. Passing the *Greek Monastery of "Mar Elias,"* the road is joined by the one connecting Bethlehem with the Old City of Jerusalem. Cut off in 1948 from Hebron Road, the Jordanians built a new road that twists up and down the mountain slopes and, though scenically beautiful, quadruples the distance between Jerusalem and Bethlehem. On the outskirts of Bethlehem, on the right-hand side of the road we pass **Rachel's Tomb.** The little building may look insignificant for such a popular place of worship, until we remember the intimacy with which Jews regard "Rachel Imenu"—our mother Rachel.

Turning left at the intersection, the road enters **Bethlehem,** a friendly little hill-side town surrounded by fertile valleys and olive groves. Mentioned in the early books of the Bible as "City in Judah," it was the home of Boaz, who married Ruth the Moabite and became the ancestor of the House of David. The road curves gently up the hill until it arrives at the *Church of the Nativity,* a fortress-like structure of gray stone. Considering the violent history of the Holy Land, it is not surprising that many churches and convents have been built with defense

The Church of the Nativity, Bethlehem

The Cave of the Machpela in Hebron

a prime consideration. The original church was built by the Emperor Constantine in the fourth century. Emperor Justinian rebuilt it in the sixth century, and the church as it stands today is in its foundations the work of his architects. The crypt of the church marks the place where Jesus was born. A few minutes' walk from the church is the *Milk Grotto,* where tradition has it that some drops of Mary's milk, when nursing her child, fell upon the rock and turned it white. Nursing mothers pray until this day in the grotto. The square and the winding alleys facing the church are occupied by the colorful market, where fruit and vegetables from the surrounding countryside are hawked side by side with mother-of-pearl and olive wood objects from the town's workshops. The latter can also be purchased in the many souvenir shops, which also feature nativity sets and such sartorial specialties as crusader jackets.

Two miles south of Bethlehem, off the road to Hebron, are three large water reservoirs on descending levels, in a lovely setting of pine trees and palms. These are called **Solomon's Pools,** and although Flavius Josephus says that King Solomon used to come here to enjoy the gardens, there is no indication that he brought the water to Jerusalem, as was done by the Roman Tenth Legion in the second century by way of a conduit. Today water from the pools, collected from rain water and from the

Nativity Square in Bethlehem

springs in the region, is still pumped to the Old City.

Before coming to Hebron, the road skirts the **Etzion Bloc,** a region with tragic associations in the modern history of Israel. In the 1940's four Jewish settlements were established in this area. In 1947–48 they succeeded in stemming the advance of the Egyptian and Jordanian armies on Jerusalem, but were wiped out in battle. Many of the settlers were killed, while the others were taken prisoner.

Hebron, 16 miles south of Bethlehem, is an Arab town inhabited by 17,000 Moslems. The Bible relates that Abraham pitched his tents here, and on the death of his wife Sara bought from Ephron the Hittite the Cave of Machpela as a burial place. Later Abraham himself was buried here, as well as Isaac, Rebecca, Leah and Jacob. According to Jewish tradition, the cave is the grave of Adam and Eve, who lived here after they were turned out of the Garden of Eden. The *Cave of Machpela* is surmounted by a fortress-like structure built by Herod the Great, to which the Mamelukes added the upper part. It contains a mosque, originally a Byzantine and later a Crusader church, named after Abraham, whom the Moslems venerate as "the Friend of God". They use the same name—*El Khalil*—for the town, rather than Hebron. Inside the mosque are cenotaphs of the patriarchs and matriarchs buried in the cave below.

Instead of returning to Jerusalem by the same way, the excursion can be extended. About three miles North of Hebron, a road turns off to the east which leads, after about 20 miles, to the **Herodium.** In the conical summit of the mountain Herod the Great built himself a fortress, where he was later buried. In comparison with the grander scale and more inaccessible surroundings of Massada, this seems only a preliminary exercise of a less megalomaniac and persecution-driven Herod, but is still worth a visit.

The road turns north again to *Beit Sahur,* a village outside Bethlehem where the *Shepherd's Field* is located, and turns east into the forbidding but beautiful Judaean desert. Soon a *fata morgana* seems to unfold itself, but fantastic as it looks, the **Mar Saba Monastery** is real and has been so for 1500 years. The Greek convent is hewn out of and clings to the steep mountainside, a micropolis of chapels, dwellings and tombs. Women are not admitted. Jerusalem is regained through the village of Abu Dis.

If the main road is taken back from Hebron to Jerusalem, the last part can be alternated by the Jordanian built road mentioned above. Turn right at the intersection after Rachel's Tomb.

DEAD-SEA—JORDAN RIVER—JERICHO

The road to Jericho starts at the Garden of Gethsemane and passes the Mount of Olives, Bethpage, Bethany and a number of villages. Soon, however, it leaves all signs of civilization behind as it winds its way between the arid mountains of the Judaean desert from 2500 feet above sea level to 1200 feet below. The Dead Sea itself is described elsewhere in this guide; here, at the northern end, the main point of interest is **Qumran,** where in 1947 and subsequent years the famous Dead Sea scrolls, on display in the Shrine of the Book of Jerusalem, were discovered. The scrolls constitute Biblical and other texts of the Essenes who had a settlement here, the remains of which have been excavated and can be visited. They kept the scrolls in nearby caves, where they were found by Bedouins.

Jericho is one of the oldest, if not the oldest, cities in the world. Excavations have laid bare 23 different strata, the oldest of which is 10,000 years old. It is also the lowest city in the world at 1200 feet below sea level. The town is surrounded by lush fruit plantations and its streets are lined with red flowering poinciana trees. This abundant flora, so unexpected in the arid

An oasis near the city of Jericho

Jordan valley, is due to the *Spring of Elisha,* which gushes forth in the middle of the town. The name refers to Elisha, disciple of the prophet Elijah, who made the bitter waters of the spring palatable by casting a handful of salt into it. Opposite the spring are the *Excavations of the Tel* (mound) with the 23 strata, carried out during 15 years by the archaeologist Kathleen Kenyon. Among the finds are a city wall and a circular tower dating back to 7,000 B.C.

North of the town is *Khirbet el Mafjar* or *Omayyad Palace.* These are the ruins of the palace of Caliph Hisham Ibn Abdul Malik of the Omayyad dynasty, who constructed a grandiose residence of columned courtyards, mosaic floors, fountains and baths, only to have it destroyed in 747 A.D. by an earthquake when in the final stages of construction. The most fascinating remnant is a beautiful mosaic floor depicting a fruit tree and a lion attacking gazelles. Also extremely interesting are the ornaments and decorations of the palace, which are on display in the Rockefeller Museum in Jerusalem.

West of Jericho the **Mount of Temptation** rises abruptly from the plain. Here Jesus was tempted by the devil after fasting for forty days. A Greek Orthodox monastery clings to the steep mountain side.

Leaving Jericho in easterly direction, a road leads straight to the point in the *Jordan River* where John the Baptist baptized Jesus. The site is also accepted as the spot where the Children of Israel crossed the river on their way to the promised land. Various churches have chapels here for the use of the many pilgrims who visit the location.

SEBASTE

This interesting archaeological site can be visited on a half-day tour from Jerusalem. It can also be reached from Jericho and thus be included in the preceding tour, or, as a third alternative, can be visited on the way from Jerusalem to the north of the country. The road northwards from Jerusalem to Nablus leads first through prosperous Arab suburbs and soon reaches *Ramallah,* a favorite summer resort with many small hotels and pensions. From here the road winds through a rustic landscape of small villages, vineyards and vegetable plots. These are the hills of Judaea and, a bit further north, of Samaria, full of Biblical associations. Forty miles north of Jerusalem you reach *Nablus,* a city of 90,000 inhabitants and capital of Samaria. It is situated between *Mount Gerizim* and *Mount Ebal,* where Joshua assembled the twelve tribes of Israel. Mount Gerizim is the sanctuary of the Samaritans, who separated from the Jews after the exile in Babylon. Today they number only a few hundred and live in Nablus and Holon near Tel Aviv. The drive up the mountain is worthwhile because of the beautiful view of the whole region. On the outskirts of Nablus is *Jacob's Well*, named after the Patriarch who tended his herds here. It also marks the site where Jesus met the Samaritan woman and asked her for water. Various churches have been built over the well during the ages. The present one, Greek Orthodox, is still under construction.

Continuing northwards, you reach the entrance to **Sebaste** after six miles. You drive up to the Arab village of the same name, and set out on foot to visit the extensive excavations. The city of Samaria (Shomron in Hebrew) was founded by King Omri in the ninth century B.C. as capital of the Israelite (Northern) Kingdom. His son Ahab (who shares his reputation for evil with his wife Jezebel) continued the building program on such a luxurious scale that he brought down the ire of the prophets upon himself. The city was conquered by the Assyrians in 720 B.C. and its inhabitants taken into exile. It rose to greatness once more in the first century B.C. under the scepter of Herod the Great, who rebuilt it on a grandiose scale and renamed it Sebaste in honor of the emperor Augustus, using the Greek equivalent of his name. The more spectacular structures to be excavated thus far are those built by Herod and include a temple of enormous proportions, a theater and a colonnaded street. The Crusader church in the village itself houses a tomb reputed to be that of John the Baptist.

Returning to the main road, you go either north to the Jezreel Valley and Galilee or south to Jerusalem, depending on your destination.

CHAPTER *6*

WHAT TO SEE IN ISRAEL

Although Israel is a small country, there is still much to see. It can be covered hurriedly in days and fairly well in weeks. Distances to an American accustomed to hundreds of miles' driving, will be preposterously small despite the fact that there are no super highways or overhead passes in towns. But, again, Israel is not the type of country in which you "burn up the road" unless you want to miss a treasure trove.

The excursions suggested here will take you around the country, and leave you with a vivid impression of its past and present landmarks. They range from half- to two-day trips, some can be extended, others comfortably combined.

AROUND TEL AVIV AND JAFFA

Tel Aviv is all present, Jaffa mostly of the past. Few twins have ever been so dissimilar. Tel Aviv, "The Hill of Spring" in translation, was a sand dune fifty-six years ago. Jaffa, the "Yafo" or "Joppa" of antiquity, was named after Japheth, son of Noah, who established the town after the Great Flood. Skeptics who doubt this claim can at least settle for proof of Jaffa's pre-history by consulting the ancient Egyptian records in which it is mentioned even before the Twelve Tribes entered Canaan.

Remains of a Roman statue at Caesarea

Tel Aviv is the most convenient hub of any Israel visit. If you arrive at Lod by air, it is twenty minutes away; from Haifa port it is an hour distant.

Israel's own pioneer fathers with their strong Puritan tradition, may sometimes think of Tel Aviv as a modern Sodom, but you will smile at the appellation, scarcely earned by a few modest night clubs or hotels with bars and floor shows. As yet there is no casino in Israel although the pros and cons have been debated for some time now. Only in recent years, in part an expression of the new generation, of a rising standard of living and of tourism, have the hard glitter and easier virtue of Europe's main cities appeared. It can be seen around Dizengoff Circle where the sophistication and dress of the young women match anything in the West and around the bars and lounges of some of the hotels.

But Tel Aviv is first and foremost a hard-working city for all the host of seafront cafés, bright shops, and crowded beaches. It contains much of Israel's light industry, commerce, and banking, and in its own right, is a modest port. Its character is also reflected in a serious cultural bent. In few places are theaters, concerts, and museums better attended, and political and intellectual pursuits more intense.

Of all places in Israel, Tel Aviv is not one where you should seek history. In its short life, this erstwhile suburb of Jaffa exploded into a white, formless metropolitan mass. The main boulevards and shopping center, originally clustered around Allenby Road, have long been left behind by the incessant building of square white apartment blocks and houses northwards as far as the Yarkon River. Greater Tel Aviv now has a population of 600,000 compared with 40,000 in 1914.

Tel Aviv, then, is not a city to look at—but rather a city to enjoy. You can swim in its Mediterranean waters, lie on its beaches, boat on the Yarkon River, and sample the shops, theaters, cafés, and concerts in the beautiful new Mann Auditorium. Not that Tel Aviv is completely devoid of sights that intrigue the sightseer. Works of old and new masters are shown at the *Tel Aviv Museum* and the *Helena Rubinstein Pavilion of Modern Art,* while the *Ha'aretz Museum* conducts exhibitions of ancient glassware, coins and pottery. But taken as a whole, Tel Aviv is not a Rome, or a Paris—if a comparison were to be made to a Western city, Los Angeles would be the best example.

The harbor of **Jaffa** is one of the oldest in the world. Here is where the cedars of Lebanon brought by Solomon to build his Temple were unloaded. A Jewish legend has it that "all the silver, gold and precious stones wrecked with the ships in all seas flow to Jaffa. In this way was Solomon delivered most of his wealth. The treasure accumulating in the sea since then will be apportioned to the righteous, each according to his merits, with the coming of the Messiah."

Among the pilgrims who have stepped reverently upon Jaffa's shores was the prophet Jonah who from here began the journey which culminated in his ride in the whale. Later the city was a stronghold of the Maccabees, and still later an Arab and a Crusader seaport. In 1799 it was besieged and completely destroyed by Napoleon. Outside Tel Aviv, at Ramat Gan, is Napoleon's Hill where he encamped. Excavations here have uncovered ruins of an ancient unidentified city.

Old Jaffa stands on a hill above the harbor, and from the top there is a superb view of Tel Aviv and the Mediterranean coast. The ancient harbor and fortifications are but a fraction of Jaffa's endless antiquity. Most of the relics of history are still buried beneath the debris and await systematic excavation which, in turn, awaits adequate funds. In the meantime, the religious sites draw many visitors.

The Great Mosque, called Mahmudiye after its builder, a famous Jaffa Governor of the 19th century, was built in 1810. It stands to the right of a square dominated by a stone tower at the end of Tarshish Street.

The Franciscan *Monastery of St. Peter* is at the top of the hill. St. Peter often visited Jaffa, and it was here that the widow Tabitha was brought back to life.

According to Christian tradition, the *house of Simon the tanner* where St. Peter's miracles took place stood on the site of the little mosque in a narrow alley close to the monastery. Dating from 1730, the mosque is the earliest in Jaffa.

The old city, once crumbling and dilapidated, a refuge for underworld characters, has been turned into a delightful art and entertainment center. The jumble of houses with their characteristic courtyards, staircases, roof terraces and vaulted ceilings have been repaired and cleaned up and let as artist studios, art galleries, craft shops, cafes, restaurants and night clubs. A stroll through the winding, climbing alleys becomes an enchanting exploration tour. During the day, the blue Mediterranean provides a refreshing background, at night unobtrusive lighting supplies a romantic touch. Even the newly installed water pipes running along the house facades have been sheathed in stone in order not to spoil the appearance of the quarter.

For unsophisticated shopping and some real old-fashioned bargaining there is the near-by flea market.

REHOVOT — RAMLE — LYDDA

The 14-mile drive to Rehovot takes you through some of the earliest towns and villages settled by Israel's pioneers. About half way you come to *Rishon le Zion,* settled, as the name suggests, by "the First in Zion" about eighty years ago in the face of the most incredible difficulties offered by the Turks. Part of the city legend is the story, unquestionably true, that when the early citizens decided to erect the present synagogue, officials were bribed to obtain a permit to build a warehouse, and when the Turkish Governor was around, sacks, barrows and stores filled the house of prayer. Rishon is famed for its wine cellars, the most extensive the country has, and their "Carmel" products have made sizeable inroads on the world market.

Two miles down the road will bring you to *Nes Ziona,* a village of the same vintage, which takes pride in being the first place where the flag of Zion was unfurled.

Another few miles and you reach **Rehovot** and its world-renowned scientific center. *The Weizmann Institute of Science,* named for Israel's first president, is a truly tremendous achievement for so tiny a land. Often asked how so small a country, desolate and limited in natural resources, could be expected to take in millions of dispersed Jews, Dr. Chaim Weizmann answered with one word—"Science."

Dr. Weizmann was in all sense a remarkable man: a statesman of international repute who fought the political battle for the formation of the State of Israel, his abiding love was science and research. The Institute, established on his 70th birthday by friends and admirers, was the dream project of his life.

In the thirty years since, it has grown to include departments for Applied Mathematics, Biophysics, Electronics, Nuclear Physics, Isotopes, Organic Chemistry, Plant Genetics, Microbiology, and many other fields. Of the greatest importance to Israel is the applied research carried out on local problems of agricultural and industrial development. The Agricultural Experimental Station, for instance, has developed strains of coffee and wheat with startling yields. Another recent discovery was a new process for making "heavy water" for the production of fuel for atomic

The A. and E. Wix Auditorium of the Weizmann Institute of Science

power. In addition to the scientific buildings, with such show pieces as the electronic brains and De Graaf Atom Smasher, the beautiful campus of woodland, flowers and lawns, houses a first-rate modern library and a charming residential area for the scientific staff.

A glance at the visitors' book of the Institute will convey why Rehovot means so much for the present and future, not only for Israelis. Hundreds of the most recent signatures include those of representatives of new African and Asian countries who in 1960 took part in a conference on the use of science for the advancement of developing nations. One of its decisions was to set up a permanent body, its center at the Weizmann Institute.

The next stop, **Ramle,** is again far back in the past. Although today it is a Jewish city with a small minority of Christian and Moslem Arabs, it was established in 716 A.D. by the Caliph Suleiman, and is the only Arab-founded town in Israel. For hundreds of years it was the capital of Palestine, and at its peak noted for its beauty and prosperity. Ramle is a busy, though not beautiful, road and rail link on the way south to Jerusalem, with some notable monuments.

St. Nicodemus is a lovely Franciscan monastery and church. Napoleon is said to have stayed in the monastery in his 1799 Palestine campaign. According to medieval Christian tradition, the town of Rama or Ramonla stood on the site of the present Ramle, and it was from here that came St. Joseph of Arimathaea who arranged the burial of Jesus.

The Great Mosque, originally a Crusaders' church from the 12th century, stands in the center of the town. A nearby street leads to the *Tower of Ramle,* sometimes called the Tower of the Forty, a beautiful example of Arab art of the 14th century. Surrounding the tower are the ruins of a Saracen castle, once an important station for caravans traveling between Syria and Egypt and between Jaffa and Jerusalem. You can visit the subterranean vaults used as storehouses.

The Pool of St. Helena is close to the monastery. This reservoir or cistern was built in the 8th century to hold the town's water supply.

En route back to Tel Aviv, digress slightly to make one more stop at **Lydda (Lod).** Again, chiefly a Jewish town with some Arab citizens, Lydda is another of those towns with origins so ancient they are lost in obscurity. Mentioned in Egyptian hieroglyphics 3,500 years ago, known to have been fortified in Joshua's time, Lydda was later rebuilt by descendants of the tribe of Benjamin.

One of Lydda's native sons is believed to be St. George, Patron Saint of England, who served in the Roman army and was martyred during the reign of Diocletian. He was brought back to be buried in his birthplace. *The Church of St. George* was built in the last century on the remnants of a 12th-century Crusader basilica which, in turn, rests on an older ruin of 6th-century Byzantine vintage. Resting on another part of the same foundations of the original cathedral is a mosque.

In the crypt is the empty tomb of St. George covered with a stone sculptured in relief. Under the mosque adjoining the church are further Byzantine and Crusader remains.

THE CITIES

OF THE

PHILISTINES

Be it short or long, the itinerary of any visit rarely omits **Ashkelon.** Even today, so far removed from the endless centuries of its history, it is easy to understand why it has been constantly coveted by conquerors. Thirty-seven miles south of Tel Aviv, Ashkelon has always stood on the legendary Via Maris, the ancients' road to the sea. Throughout history it has flourished as a port and built a tradition of opulence and splendor. It has been the home of various civilizations of antiquity, including Philistine, Egyptian, Hebrew, Greek, Roman, Byzantine, and Early Arab, as well as others much nearer to our times.

History literally bestrews the silvery sand of Ashkelon's shore. For miles around you find the fragments of paper thin colored glass left by the Phoenicians, pieces of earthen pottery, and the chunks of stone and pillar upon which this endless history rests. A walk along the beach is a fitting introduction to this, one of the five most important Philistine cities, the only one built on the coast with a major harbor. You will feel impelled to stoop almost every yard to burrow amid the sand for at least a Greek or Roman coin, a Hebrew seal, a piece of Egyptian mosaic, and it may even happen that you will be lucky.

Lady Hester Lucy Stanhope began excavating the site of ancient Ashkelon at the end of the 19th century because of the popular belief that great treasures still rest beneath its soil. Most of the finds so far were dug up in 1920–21, bringing to light the remains of various buildings, statues and columns. Since then, excavation has been limited and sporadic despite the fact that only the tiniest percentage of what existed has yet been found. You will meet inhabitant after inhabitant of modern Ashkelon who will tell you that when he turned over his garden soil for the first time, he found this or that coin, an Aladdin lamp, or pieces of an ancient vase, and invite you in to see his private collection. No one was surprised when the bulldozers, pushing out a road to the tract of land called *Barnea,* struck and revealed the ruins of a Philistine temple by the sea.

As to the written or painted history in its various forms, there is just no end to it. On the wall of a palace of Ramses II, King of Egypt in the 13th century B.C., amid the ruins of Karnak, is carved a picture of Ashkelon on a hill. In the wall surrounding the buttressed town are two gates and Egyptian soldiers are storming the city. A hieroglyph inscription reads: "The wretched which his majesty captured when it rebelled Ashkelon."

Under Roman rule the city was famed for its splendid buildings. King Herod the Great was born here. During the time of the Crusades, Ashkelon was an important fortress city, savagely fought for by both Christians and Moslems. Richard the Lion Hearted took the city in 1191. It was finally destroyed a century later by the Mameluke Sultan Beibars.

Some of the ruins of this long history survive. Among the places that should be visited are: *The Ancient City Site* where three statues of the Goddess of Victory form the centerpiece of uncovered foundations of various buildings surrounded by the ancient wall which protrudes from the sand; *The Philistine Harbor,* half a mile away strewn across a mound overlooking the coast, with its surviving granite pillars, reservoir and other remains; *The Painted Burial Cave* near the bathing beach, depicting goddesses,

A few of the hundreds of "finds" collected in the Ashkelon Antiquities Park

gorgons, vines, Pan, and other mythological themes, its vault dating back to the Roman period; *The Local Museum,* which contains relics of all ages.

New Ashkelon, built in 1953, is a showpiece of modern town planning with gardens, lawns and fountain in front of the cultural and shopping center. Along the paths and lacing the pleasant green, are segments of pillars and stone engravings from the ancient city. New Ashkelon is a summer resort for people from other parts of the country. Many of the technicians and skilled workers of the northern Negev live here, as do employees of the nearby Yuval Gad Pipe Factory which makes the gigantic pre-stressed concrete lines and conduits for the national irrigation networks.

About 9 miles north of Ashkelon on the coastal plain is **Ashdod,** a Philistine stronghold in Biblical times. Little remains of the ancient city. It is known however, that this was the site of the great Temple of Dagon, half-fish, half-man, to which was brought the sacred Ark the Philistines had taken from the Israelites. In Samuel we read: "And the Philistines took the ark of God, and brought it from Eben-ezer unto Ashdod. When the Philistines took the ark of God, they brought it into the house of Dagon, and set it by Dagon. And when they of Ashdod arose early on the morrow, behold, Dagon was fallen upon his face to the earth before the ark of the Lord. And they took Dagon, and set him in his place again. And when they arose early on the morrow morning, behold, Dagon was fallen upon his face to the ground before the ark of the Lord; and the head of Dagon and both the palms of his hands were cut off upon the threshold; only the stump of Dagon was left to him. Therefore neither the priests of Dagon, nor any that come into Dagon's house, tread on the threshold of Dagon in Ashdod unto this day."

Modern Ashod is a new town (25,000 inhabitants) with an even newer deep-sea harbor, which provides the southern part of the country with a port from which to ship citrus fruit and chemicals from the Negev.

If you are interested in such furious development activity, which, after all, is one of the central themes of Israel's current existence, you will want to stop at Ashod on your way to or from Ashkelon. When the dust and clamor of construction settles at Ashod and people get used to living in it, excavation of the archaeological type will most probably be tackled as well. No doubt pieces will in the meantime appear by accident rather than design.

It is neither history nor archaeology that draws the swarm of visitors to **Kiryat Gat** and the **Lachish Regional Settlement Zone** some 15 miles east of Ashkelon. True, Gat and the ruins of almost eternal Lachish are among the most exciting discoveries that have corroborated the written record of the Bible. But it is highly doubtful whether the thousands of Africans and Asians who have made a pilgrimage to Lachish since 1957 are even aware of the Biblical finds. What brings them here are the experiments in town planning that the Israel government has set up here in this arid desert terrain.

In Gat itself you will find an excellent public relations office. On one wall is a huge map of 54 villages of the project which radiate out from Gat like the spokes of a wheel. Even if you are not a sociologist or anthropologist or town planner or some other kind of expert, you will be fascinated by the Lachish story.

Its ingredients are a 100,000-acre slice of wilderness and about 45,000 people, most of them untrained immigrants from North Africa and the Middle East. Add to this a core of experts and veteran pioneers, and a vast adventure through planning in getting people of various backgrounds, languages, habits and cultures to work and *live* together. Results have been so successful and original that the Lachish techniques are being copied in lands as far away as Burma, Nepal, Ethiopia, and Nigeria.

A quick look at Gat and its surrounding villages will tell you that this is something different, even in Israel terms. You will see groups of six villages sharing central services instead of each community having its own. Instead of each village containing people from many countries, as in the rest of Israel, you will find that the settlers in those of Lachish are from one land only, often from the same Moroccan, Iranian or Yemenite town or village.

On the western outskirts of the Lachish development, of which Kiryat Gat is the center, you find excavations at the ancient site have thrown light on Biblical Lachish itself and on life during the entire period. You reach them from the main road by following a dirt track to the hill called *Tell ed-Duweir* in Arabic. This

New housing for workers in Kiryat Gat

is the site of Lachish, at the beginning of the regional settlement group of villages.

This ancient fortified city—stamped out of existence even before Roman times, had a long and violent history. The Bible mentions it often—almost always as a city besieged or as an army headquarters. The archaeological activities in this area began in 1933 by the English Wellcome and Marston expedition. By the time the leader of the group, John Starkey, was killed in 1937, a great many important finds had been made, the most critical being the *Lachish Letters*. These letters, written on clay tablets to the governor of the city-fort during the latter part of the 6th century B.C. have been of great use to scholars of the period.

On your return from the Lachish excavations, you will find the ruins of Biblical *Gat* on the Beit Guvrin road. Birthplace of the giant Goliath, this was the Philistine city captured by David, and from which the musical instrument *gittith* originated.

Excavations at the foot and on top of the mound of Gat were started in 1957-59, and the foundations of clay-brick buildings, potsherds, and Hebrew seals on jar handles of the Judaean period were found.

A few miles further on is the kibbutz of **Beit Guvrin.** Like so many other Israeli settlements, it stands on historic ground. It was an important Roman town, and later a Crusader stronghold called Gibelin. Its main claim to fame today as a tourist attraction are the fabulous and beautiful mosaic floors which can be seen in the *Roman villa* unearthed in 1924. There are three of them, each from a different period, ranging from the 2nd to the 6th century A.D.

Just over a mile away to the south, across the main road are the ruins of **Mareisha**, the ancient city which preceded Beit Guvrin to prominence in the area. Originally fortified by Rehoboam, son of Solomon, Mareisha was the birthplace of both Micah and Eliezer. It was destroyed by the Parthians. There are several burial caves, some of them enormous, near Mareisha, linked together with passageways, which can be visited. It is believed that these caves were in use originally as shelter long before Biblical times. The rooms have carved niches in the wall which held funeral urns.

South of Ashkelon. A tour of the three Philistine cities and the surrounding area may be supplemented by visits to two villages on the approaches to the Egyptian-held Gaza Strip whose names every Israeli knows because of the part they played in the 1948 war: Negba and Yad Mordekhai. Negba, for instance, is on the road back to Ashkelon, and Yad Mordekhai is five miles south of the port. These were the two frontier outposts which stopped the armor and infantry, supported by planes, of the Egyptians, with light weapons and unbounded courage. *Negba's* buildings were completely flattened by artillery during the fighting; but the kibbutz, though overrun, was never abandoned. Evidence of its struggle can be seen in its battered white watertower kept as a reminder of the fighting and the cemetery with its war memorial. *Yad Mordekhai,* named after Mordekhai Anilevits, leader of the Warsaw Ghetto revolt against the Nazis during World War II, is but two miles north of the Gaza Strip border. During the 1948 war it was one of the first targets of the Egyptians. The defenders held out against forces outnumbering them by more than ten to one until finally forced to draw back.

Both villages are of the collective type, their lands owned and worked by the entire community on the principle: "From each according to his means to each according to his need."

THE NEGEV
AND THE
DEAD SEA

BEERSHEBA

Most Israelis look disdainful when you talk of Beersheba as the Negev. For them the triangular desert with the salt-infested soil or sand and the burnt-up mountains begins south of its capital city. Nevertheless, the better soil and clime of the Beersheba plain, which rolls from the Mediterranean eastwards to the Dead Sea and is cradled from north to south between the Judaean and Negev highlands, is historically, geographically, and in every other way, the Negev. What Israelis really mean is that to live or even travel south of Beersheba is to be in tough pioneer country—north of it life is soft. Their fathers probably held the same view as they ventured into the Jezreel and Jordan swamps of the north. Anyone in the coastal plain then was less than a pioneer.

What the Israeli sometimes forgets is that Beersheba and its plain in 1948 were almost completely desolate and uninhabited. Although yet far from completely settled, Beersheba has been transformed in less than fifteen years from wasteland to a place capable of supporting 100,000 people.

Before you reach Beersheba on the road from the north, the Bedouin village of *el-Huzeil* sprawls to the left, the domain of the oft-publicized Sheikh Suleiman of the 39 wives and 200 camels. Besides heading the biggest Bedouin tribe of the Negev's 15,000 nomads, this opulent son of the desert has made his encampment a tourist magnet. His is the large stone house at the entrance. Many of the black goat-haired tents in the background shelter his 39 wives and countless offspring. The Suleiman encampment shares a dam and reservoir with the contrastingly settled kibbutz village of *Shoval* across the road.

At this point you are 17 miles from Beersheba and about to cross the Gerar brook which is the northern Negev border. On your left is *Mishmar Hanegev*—Watchguard of the Negev—one of the first pioneer villages to penetrate the area and the site of a large Nabatean cemetery and cistern. These ancient expert water engineers (c. 220 B.C.–105 A.D.) have taught Israel's present hydrologists a lot about how to fight a desert. This cistern, hewn with chisels out of limestone rock, is as large as a hall and placed just at the right spot to catch winter flood water rushing down from the surrounding hills. Near it is a large modern reservoir, the difference between life or death for the village.

Beersheba sits dead center of the plain, a white outgrowth amid the dun which someone called "a poached egg on toast." When you enter the city, there will be one disappointment. Most people arrive with the thought at the back of their minds they are coming to a frontier outpost, something like the wild and woolly West. This was true as late as the early fifties when everything had that scorched, parched look and houses were surrounded by sand. Today Beersheba has 50,000 inhabitants, a blueprint to bring in 50,000 more, and a green belt of trees and gardens fast enveloping its raw carpet. The original Beersheba, which was not much more than two narrow streets of old stone houses in 1948, is hidden away by blocks of multi-storied apartment buildings. And as you tour the town, you will soon become aware of the growing industrial belt, the network of oil and rail lines coming up from the deeper Negev.

Many of the institutions in Beersheba will remind you it is the capital city of the region. Here are grouped the *District Court* which has usurped the traditional role of Bedouin chieftains who used to be judge and jury to their tribes, and the clinics and hospitals which use medicine and science as a balm for illness in place of superstition. Every Thursday morning, when the Bedouins hold market day, you will see the crowd of nomads waiting for treatment outside the clinic, their donkeys and camels parked nearby. Not all are ill—the clinic as a place of gossip and chit-chat is the new version of the village well. The much advertised

Bedouin Market, where camel meat, dead and alive, wool, eggs, and other nomad products are sold and bartered for modern gewgaws, deserves a visit of a few hours. Bedouin women, heavily garbed in black, their faces veiled, foreheads covered by threaded coins, squat around the stalls, while their dashing menfolk do the bargaining.

Most interesting of all Beersheba's modern sights is the campus of the *Arid Zone Research Institute* which is science's G.H.Q. in the fight to conquer the desert. Here is the prototype of a solar energy generator which already has made world news, and perhaps will make history. Nearby are the ecological gardens where the plants and shrubs of the Negev and other deserts are grown and crossed. On another part of the grounds experiments are being conducted with a solar powered refrigerator. Other experiments are in progress concerned with desalination, the effects of desert climate on man's body, and the possibility of using ocean water for irrigation.

HIAS House for technicians and officials passing through is an interesting place to lunch or dine, for here you can meet and hear the key experts upon whose shoulders the various burdens of desert reclamation fall.

Another place to lounge is the attractively modern *Beit Ha'am,* containing municipal offices, the tourist information office, restaurant, swimming pool and bar.

Among the industries, a tour of the *Harsa Ceramics Plant* is rewarding. It is turning out, for home and foreign markets, all sorts of ornaments of the newest designs from materials quarried further south.

If you spend the evening in Beersheba, the place assumes an entirely different character. Cafés which looked mundane by day suddenly light up their attached gardens in many colors, and every type of music from oriental to twist blares out in the streets. It seems the entire populace has congregated in the town center, and here you will see the characteristic mixture of East

Potash works near Sodom on the Dead Sea

European and North African newcomers crowding everywhere. One unique place of entertainment is the *Sheikh's Tent* at the Desert Inn Hotel. A Bedouin tent (real) provides the setting for this night club, and the culinary specialties as well as the entertainment are distinctly Oriental.

In the city of the patriarchs you can expect to find historic sights. The most interesting found to date are of a period 1,000 years before Abraham. The French archaeologist Jean Perrot uncovered a chain of subterranean villages of a culture which existed across the northern Negev approximately 6,000 years ago. Astonishing is the fact that these Chalcolithic inhabitants of Beersheba grew wheat and barley, brought copper from over 60 miles south, wrought weapons and ornaments from it, and carried on a busy trade between Mesopotamia and Egypt. It is believed they came from Anatolia or thereabouts. Some of the remarkable finds of the period are in the local archaeological museum—the excavations are at *Abu Matar*, on the southern bank of the Beersheba brook, a few miles from the town.

Of the Abrahamic period, all that has been discovered is a *well* at the end of *Keren Kayemet Street* which is attributed to the patriarch and called by his name. Remains of the time of the Judaean Kingdom and Christian remnants from the 5th century have also been found in the vicinity.

SODOM AND THE DEAD SEA

The drive from Beersheba to the Dead Sea via Arad is 45 miles, half of it epic in scenery. (Arad can also be reached from Jerusalem via Hebron.)

Arad. 30 miles distant, is a brand new Negev town that has shot up in the last few years. Located at an altitude of 1500 feet, it enjoys a cool, dry climate. This, together with its proximity to the Dead Sea, where the heat makes for uncomfortable living conditions, makes it an ideal base for workers in the Dead Sea industries. The town is also developing its own industries based on minerals found in the region, and is becoming a tourist center serving patients taking treatment at the Dead Sea.

The road to the Dead Sea is an unprecedented testimony to the enginering prowess of the Israel Defense Army. Literally cut through mountains, and in parts a ridge along cliff sides, the highway winds steeply downward to the lowest part of the earth's surface. Thousands of laborers—immigrants and local Bedouins—built it in the intense heat, so fierce nearest the sea that shifts had to be short, followed by long rest periods.

When first you sight the *Dead Sea* lying far below, you will notice that it is covered by a kind of fog—caused by the intense evaporation. Level with the murky gray of the viscous water is a vast dead tableland, whitened by its surface of salt. This vast desert plain stretches eastward to the foot of the high mountain range of Edom and Moab in Jordan. This is the *Arava,* divided from north to south by a border between Israel and Jordan as far as the Red Sea.

The Sea, which lies 1,286 feet below sea level, is 48 miles long, 11 at its maximum width, and in places 1,319 feet deep. Israel, under the Armistice Agreements, owns 101 square miles of it, and 35 miles of its shore. Each day, according to calculations, 6½ million tons of water fall into the sea, but it never overflows because of evaporation. The remaining water is so impregnated with salt that about 25 per cent of it is mineral substance, potash, magnesium, sodium, calcium, and other salts. Its water has an oily feeling; fish cannot live in it since it destroys nearly all organic life, but you can and should try going for a "swim." It is an experience you shouldn't miss.

Sodom, at the southern tip, is where the potash and bromide plants process the chemicals, turning them into a major export. It is also according to tradition where Sodom and Gomorrah, sym-

Salt from the Dead Sea coats the wood blown to the seashore

bols of evil, were destroyed by fire and brimstone.

A mile or so north along the seashore you will find the *Cave of Sodom* and the salt mines. Above the opening of the cavern is a pillar of salt which all Israelis insist was once Lot's wife. The road along the shore leads to the area where the most remarkable archaeological discoveries of modern times have been made.

First you come to *Hamei Zohar,* 10 miles from Sodom, where David and Solomon came every winter to bathe in the mineral springs. The medical advice of the Bible is not being ignored. A busy bath-house and clinic now stand on the site, and Israeli doctors claim great successes for the waters. Two miles further is the *Ein Bokek* guest house and bathing beach.

Another ten miles northward, along the western Dead Sea shore, and you are at the foot of **Mount Massada** rising high over the murky water. Here begins a climb into a remarkable piece of history. At the top are the magnificent ruins of the fortress where from 70 to 73 A.D. the Jewish defenders, under Eliezer Ben Yair, made the last stand of the Judaean revolt against Rome. Rather than suffer the humiliation of captivity, these warriors, their wives and children, took their own lives.

If you decide to make the climb—it is an arduous one because of the heat and the steepness of the path—arrange your schedule to give yourself three to four hours at least. It's not much more than 2 miles each way, but you will want to spend some time here once you have reached the plateau. The ascent from the west side is shorter and easier. It can be reached by car from Arad, or you can ride to the top in a cable car. There are organized tours from Arad that see to transportation and guides for the antiquities.

Although Massada had been fortified originally a century before, Herod the Great was the main builder of the remains visible today. It was he who between 37 and 30 B.C. built the massive wall enclosing the plateau, and the magnificent palace, the remains of which can still be seen. The remains of storehouses, cisterns and of a 6th century Byzantine church are also on view.

Because Massada symbolizes Jewish resistance to oppression, it has become a kind of shrine to which young Israelis make frequent pilgrimages.

Ten miles further north along the sea road brings you to **Ein Gedi** where ruins of the Judaean city and of the Essene settlements of the earliest Christians have been excavated. The community dining halls and storehouses confirm the written records of how these religious aesthetes turned• their backs on private wealth, shared everything they earned and possessed, and lived in true brotherhood. The new kibbutz village called Ein Gedi, which stands so near the Essene ruins, is a startling return

Herod's Massada, last redoubt of the Jewish resistance against Rome

to this communal type of life. It, too, has a community dining room and treasury. History, on this Dead Sea shore, has a peculiar talent for repeating itself exactly.

The fertility of the modern settlement, like that so extolled in the past, is due to *David's Fountain,* a beautiful spring cascading and foaming over the rocks. The green fields and slender palms are as startling in this parched environment as the cool, fresh water itself, and are reminiscent of various Biblical passages about the vineyards and luxuriant growth of the region.

The entire district here is a mass of forbidding cliffs and almost inaccessible caves, as numerous as the holes in a pepper pot. Recently, with the use of ropes and helicopters, archaeological expeditions led by Professor Yigal Yadin made major finds in some of them. The most publicized have been scrolls, weapons, and skeletons of the Judaean leader Simon Bar Kochba and his warriors who in 132 A.D. rose up against Rome, and liberated the whole of the country for three years. Until these finds were made, the sole proof of this uprising reposed in ancient documents. Close by were hundreds of relics of Chalcolithic man from 6,000 years ago.

Beyond Ein Gedi are the *Qumran Caves,* where the world famous Dead Sea .Scrolls were discovered by Bedouins chasing stray goats from their flock. As already mentioned, the Scrolls are on view at the Shrine of the Brook at the Israel Museum, Jerusalem.

THE SOUTHERN NEGEV

Even at the cost of repetition, it is again worth stressing that the journey to Eilat on the Red Sea should be made one way by road, the other by air. From Beersheba across the Negev to the southern port is 150 miles of reasonably good asphalt road which can be covered in a comfortable four-hour drive. You can take either a *sherut* taxi or bus, and the return flight to Lod is just a little over an hour. At Eilat are three four star and a number of comfortable hotels, should you wish to stay over and enjoy the sun, sea and scenery which have made it so popular a winter, spring, and fall resort for Israelis, as well as visitors.

South of Beersheba, the central Negev highway uncoils like the tempered blue-steel of a clock spring over earthless brown plain, rises into the broken heights and plateau land of the hills, and descends through Nubian red sandstone crags to a sparkling blue sea. For miles and miles this is the scenery which space travelers will surely encounter on lifeless planets. The roadside is littered with erosional debris, jagged bits of flint and limestone, gashes torn into the landscape by short, sharp winter floods. It is hard to imagine that following the Ice Age, this parched and arid desert was inundated swamp, thick jungle, green dense forest.

The fossilized bones of huge animals, armored and with terrifying jaws, have been found in the Negev's lunar craters. The vast deposits of phosphates mark the time when flood waters linked the Red and Mediterranean Seas hundreds of thousands of years ago.

The region was from earliest times an inter-continental artery between Asia and Europe. As such, most of the cities and settlements of various cultures which subsequently rose and declined on its surface, lined and defended its routes. The asphalt road over which you travel southwards has been laid on top of one of them. You will pass the ruins of villages, towns and cities from Canaanite to Byzantine periods, the dams and terraces of Judaeans and Nabateans who fought the desert, and of the forts which held back the ravaging nomads who preyed on their ancient caravans.

The desert dust and sand and the dryness of the climate have preserved these venerable relics of past civilizations. Many of the dams and new villages and townlets now rising are on their sites. At *Kfar Yeroham*, for example, on a rise just 20 miles south of Beersheba, are the remains of a Canaanite settlement. Its inhabitants work in the *Makhtesh Gadol* (Big Crater) where the mineral mines, glass sand, kaolin, and ochre are exploited. Mostly from Roumania, they started building their town in 1951, and draw their water from a nearby reservoir which collects winter flood rain from the hills, just as the inhabitants of the Judaean town of Yeroham did centuries before them.

Eleven miles south of the mining town is **Sdeh Boker,** started in 1952. The green of its fields is a tribute to the Nabatean spillways renovated by the pioneer settlers. This is the village where David Ben-Gurion made his home in 1953 when he resigned from office and to which he constantly returns to relax, write, and work on the farm. The resourceful inhabitants of the village make their agriculture pay. Wool shorn from their Corridale sheep which came from Australia is homespun and dyed and made into attractive rugs, blankets, and bags.

A few miles south, a dirt track leaves the road. It would attract no attention were it not for the noticeboard forbidding entrance. Signed by "The Prime Minister's Office and the Hebrew University," it warns against disturbances of the soil as "important scientific work is being conducted in the area." Of course, everyone enters.

In the valley bottom surrounded by hills is a most unusual farm. Built about 200 B.C. by Nabateans, it has been renovated by Professor Michael Evenari, a botanist of the Hebrew University. It has proven that what man did successfully a few thousand years ago can be repeated today. Using the same agricultural techniques, the professor and his team of volunteer students have grown barley, wheat, and fruit, and filled their cisterns with water in a 2-inch per year rainbelt area of the desert. To Israelis, never accepting limitations about the size of their 'cultivable area', this opens the newest of new frontiers.

Products of this farm were enjoyed centuries ago by the inhabitants of nearby *Avdat*, the Nabatean and later Byzantine city overlooking the asphalt road. Its ruined houses, churches, streets, and walls compose the best preserved archaeological ruin of six such historical Negev sites. Only the uppermost Byzantine

The granite mountains near Eilat

Nabatean irrigation system in the Negev

layers have been liberated from the mound of dirt and dust which covered and saved them for centuries. Work has begun on the Nabatean and who knows what earlier layers below. At the kiosk where entrance tickets are purchased is a black Bedouin tent. Its nomads are employed at night as watchmen.

Past the ruin is the welcome *Nabatean Inn,* its name spelled out in gay mosaics. From the rise on which it is built is a striking view of nature's utter desolation. The shapes of windswept hills and crags are like a million fortresses, battle towers, cathedrals, and even whole cities. The silence is overpowering, the nakedness illumined by the whitest of sun rays. The huge phosphate trucks, roaring as they mount the hills, are no larger than black beetles amid the majesty of this landscape. As they pass, dust eddies in their wake, stones are shaken loose from the hillsides. In a moment the silence returns.

The road 12 miles south reaches the desert townlet *Mitzpeh Ramon* (Ramon Lookout) on a hill overlooking the fantastic *Makhtesh Ramon* (Ramon Crater). This huge dent in the earth's surface was scooped out by winter floods carrying boulder and stone like sledgehammers against a meeting point of two geological formations. Ramon, storm god of the Assyrian pantheon, gave the crater its name, although there are some who believe that the Israelites who wended their way through it as they came out of Sinai likened it to the pomegranate (*rimon* in Hebrew) because of the red deposits of oxidized iron on its floor.

The highway winds down to the Ramon's bed. The only forms of vegetation are tiny tufts of wiry grass, the rest is rock and stone in a galaxy of color. Standing at the bottom of Ramon conjures visions of some long burnt-out part of hell, the towering cliffs around that cup the crater seem to hold up the sky. The only signs of life found on the floor of Ramon have been the fossils of gargantuan animals. Man has lived near its edge, for not far away, at *Mishor Haruakh,* the ruins of Judaean forts and farms have been found, and with them artifacts of the earlier Chalcolithic period.

Mitzpeh Ramon is a small mining town, as for miles southward from the crater are vast deposits of phosphates and other minerals in the Hamishar plain. In the next ten years, its growth is assured as extraction of minerals on a large scale has already begun. This is the plain which reaches as far as Sinai, its course dotted with impish, dwarf acacias.

As you descend from the Negev highlands, the black-topped road drops to the *Arava* plain and follows the border with Jordan. The first oasis in every sense of the word is *Yotvata* (65 miles from Mitzpeh Ramon), a frontier village pushing its own green circle of newly-made fields and palms outward in an ever-widening arc. All of its first inhabitants were army–trained, young people in their early twenties who, like their forebears, guarded the border and highway against ravaging nomads. Archaeology made this village possible for nearby were discovered the ruins of the Roman caravan inn called Ghadian, and it was assumed that sweet water could be found. Wells sunk here supply not merely Yotvata, but also the copper plant at Timna and Eilat further south.

Archaeology made its greatest practical contribution to Israel's modern economy when Nelson Glueck found Solomon's copper mines at **Timna.** References in the Bible to the Kenites, famed coppersmiths of the region, and the miracle staff of Moses with a head made of the metal, led him to the find. The present plant stands near the very slag heaps deposited there thousands of years ago by the miners of the Judaean Kingdom. When you visit Timna, however, please refrain from seeking obvious answers to obvious questions as the engineers are pestered by thousands of visitors per month obsessed by Solomon.

If you have never visited a copper plant, Timna is a good place to start. The ore is mined, crushed, and processed here, and the finished product is copper cement, 75 per cent pure. Around is some of the most enchanting scenery the country can offer, not to mention the carpet of varied-colored stones from which semi-precious jewels are cut and polished. Choose carefully with the cost of overweight air baggage in mind. One of the outstanding sights in the area are the *Amudei Shlomo*—Pillars of Solomon— sculptured by nature from Nubian sandstone.

Just before Eilat, you come to the Gadna youth camp of *Be'er Ora* where high school youth come for fortnightly work-vacations right through the summer. On the hills all around it are the names of the groups painted in huge white or colored letters whilst the fields proclaim the pioneer stress of Be'er Ora's education. This, too, is a special kind of oasis.

Journey's end comes into sight with the blue sparkle of the Red Sea. Israel shares this beauty of bay and mountains with Jordan, Egypt, and Saudi Arabia. From here out to the Indian Ocean is the narrow waterway over which the Tarshish freighters of Solomon bore their cargoes of copper and timber, and returned with "gold, and silver, ivory, and apes, and peacocks." Their port was Etzion Gever, not far from the present Eilat, named after Elah of the Edomites, so far does it date back in time.

Despite all this history, Israel's modern **Eilat** arose on an empty beach with no ancient ruins at its feet. Its return to history was slow from 1949 to 1956, probably due to the very difficulties once encountered by Solomon. In his days an Egyptian blockade over the only route linking the Red and Mediterranean Seas (where the Suez Canal now exists) brought the Queen of Sheba across 1,200 miles of desert to test the Negev-Gulf of Akaba alternative. Satisfied that Solomon's troops had made it secure, she signed a trade agreement with the Judaean monarch and Hiram of Tyre, and Etzion Gever and Elah became famous ports.

With the lifting of the Egyptian blockade of the Gulf of Akaba in 1956, this same route of antiquity has again opened the door to trade and contact with Africa, not only for Israel but for part of ancient Tyre, today's Kingdom of Jordan. One of the countries benefiting from this trade, to carry the parallel further, is Ethiopia, the emperor of which claims descent through the Queen of Sheba from the House of David. For these and other reasons, Israelis believe the modern Eilat will become "the Haifa of the Red Sea."

Eilat already combines two distinctive features in its shaping personality. Although it is a growing port, you will also be interested in its excellent swimming and skin diving facilities, its coral seas, and enticing mountains. It has a summer climate in mid-winter, but even after the hottest day the evening can become cool or cold. With only fourteen short years of existence and its population a modest 12,000, Eilat is still very much the

A coral reef at Eilat

frontier town. A poignant reminder is its preponderance of men, although the gap is gradually closing with the influx of immigrants. As all Negev development towns, Eilat, too, has that characteristic mixture of veterans and sons of veterans and the newcomers mainly from North Africa.

Among the things worth doing while in Eilat are: a sail in a glass-bottomed boat, a visit to the tropical garden and marine museum, watching the exotic catch of fishermen as they toss an amazing variety of highly-colored fish out of their nets, a tour of the *Philip Murray Cultural Center,* and a walk to and beyond the port area as far as the "Way of the Pilgrims," which, incidentally, is thought to be the place where the Israelites crossed from Sinai.

Before departure, by road or air, remember to visit the *"Even V'Chen"* workshop or store where necklaces, brooches, and other jewelry of locally found stones are made and sold.

If you fly back over the Negev, a further dimension to its beauty will be added from on high. The severity of its desert terrain and wild unspoiled loveliness will stress even more why the region is considered such a challenge to the hardiest and most ingenious of the country's pioneers and scientists.

A second route to Eilat, and one shortening the journey by 40 miles, runs along the Jordan border. This route is an old Roman road, the only one of its kind in the country, and built on the steepest escarpment in the Negev. You can drive either straight from Ein Gedi through Hatseva, or leave the main Sodom road and drive along *Ma'ale Akravim* (Scorpion Pass) through Hatseva, and then on to **Be'er** Menuha and Eilat.

FROM
TEL AVIV
TO HAIFA

The middle of Israel is like the waist of an hour glass. At one point the land's entire width pinches down to less than ten miles. This narrow link joining the two contrasting regions lies between the political frontier with Jordan to the east and the natural western border of sand—the ebb and flow of Mediterranean tides.

People who talk too easily about Israel's need to "integrate" into the Middle East forget that this coastal plain has throughout history faced westwards and the cultures of Europe. The mountains at its back in a sense cut it off from the East. The most balanced view is that Israel, ancient or modern, helped by its Mediterranean contacts, has maintained a distinctive poise between East and West. When it "integrated" with either one, it ceased to be Israel.

The 60-mile journey northward from Tel Aviv to Haifa is thus across a sandy stage from which the ancients conducted an age-long dialogue of culture, commerce, and even war with Greek and Roman civilizations. It is a dialogue which the moderns peacefully continue. Without pause, the journey is scarcely more than an hour, for the road is fine and Haifa a worthy prize. But with Apollonia, Caesarea, and Atlit en route, not to mention the artists' village of Ein Hod, few visitors make this trip in less than twice that time. Besides, this is a Mediterranean shore where sun, sand, and sea offer a constant temptation to leave the road.

Apollonia. The first reminder of Israel's eternal Mediterranean rôle is about 8 miles along the coastal road not far from the modern town of *Herzliya.* Here are the ruins of Rishpon of the Canaanites on which the Greeks built their Apollonia. The remains you see are of a *Greek period fortress,* replete with walls and moats, and of their ancient *harbor.*

Twelve miles further north is **Natanya,** flanked by a strip of almost pure white sand. This is suntan landscape at its best, but if this is your first full exposure to the hot sun's rays, make it a short interlude. When you leave this flawless beach, the attractive parks overhanging the shore are a restful green change from the golden glare. You will find the citizens of this resort town are justly proud of their *open-air amphitheater,* where plays and concerts are performed. Apart from the sun's sparkle, diamonds add luster to the town's economy, for here is where more of the stones are cut and polished than almost anywhere except in Antwerp and New York.

A few miles east of Natanya is the *Sharon Crossroad,* halfway to Haifa and the middle of the Sharon Plain. The fertile earth of this area has made it one of the most densely populated in this densely populated country. Orchards and vineyards dot the countryside. Every acre of land is made to serve a useful purpose. None is wasted. This is land that until little more than thirty years ago had for centuries been covered with sand or sunk in boggy swamps. Israeli pioneers drained the swamps and pushed back the sand dunes until now the land flourishes and produces as it did in the days of Solomon.

Ancient Roman seawall at Caesarea

Hadera, 8 miles north of the Sharon Crossroad, and a city of some 25,000, was founded in 1890 by the same pioneers who cleared the land. Mainly eastern Europeans from Poland, Lithuania, and Russia, they lived through decades of fearful hardship and toil, struggling with the swamps and the sand, weakened by overwork and malaria. The country you see around you here is a tribute to their toil. Hadera today is an important road and rail junction, as well as a market and industrial center.

Your first sight of **Caesarea** brings you something you hardly expect in Israel—a real live golf course. When Abba Eban teed off the first ball, the press wrote about it for weeks. This is not the first time sport has featured in this archaeologically opulent site. The course scarcely ends and a vast horse racing *hippodrome* left by the Romans begins. Beyond the hippodrome, which accommodated 20,000 spectators in its Roman heyday are colossal 2nd- and 3rd-century statues.

Caesarea was founded by Herod the Great some time between 20 and 10 B.C. and was the Romans' capital city until the 5th century. The Jewish rebellion of 66–73 A.D. which ended with the fall of Massada, began in Caesarea. During the Crusades, the city, considerably smaller than it had been in the days of the Romans, became one of the fortified outposts of these adventurers. Captured in 1102 by the Franks, it changed hands several times and was finally demolished by El Achraf in 1291. In the later years of Roman rule, Caesarea had been a center of Christian teaching; and when Baudouin I took the city, he is supposed to have found here the Holy Grail, the cup used at Christ's Last Supper. Except for temporary settlements by migrant peoples, Caesarea lay dormant to all intents and purposes until the Israeli kibbutz of *Sdot Yam* was founded near the site in 1940.

The excavated ruins around Caesarea are plentiful. Portions of the wall built by Herod nearly 2,000 years ago are visible, as are many finely sculptured stone columns which once adorned the walls of the ancient city's buildings. The Crusader fortifications, now restored, may be visited. The Roman theater is the site of the annual Israel Festival.

If you are interested in pre-history, you will want to visit in the area, the *cave of Kabara* where the archaeologist Moshe Stekelis found the abode and relics of prehistoric man; and not far away, the *Carmel Caves,* inhabited during the Stone Age, and excavated in 1929–34 by the British School of Archaeology and the American Institute of Pre-History. On the other hand, if Caesarea and its ancient sites have supplied sufficient shade and substance of the past, you will head directly for **Ein Hod**—"The Fount of Splendor"—the interesting artists' village which lies on a small promontory on the side of Mount Carmel. If you have never tried to paint or draw, the view from this old and abandoned Arab village taken over by the artists will make you want to begin. Below is the sea, above the mountain, and the stone houses seem hewn from its rock.

Ein Hod was started as a community of painters, poets, sculptors and writers, and not as an exhibition piece for visitors. It rose in response to their urge to create and live together. The main income of the village is derived from exhibitions and sales of artwork to the constant flow of local and foreign visitors. Some of the country's leading artists—such as Marcel Janco, Moshe Mokady, the sculptor Rudolph Lehmann, and the sculptress Shoshanna Heimann—live there most or part of the year, and their houses as well as their work are both original and colorful.

Of Israel's many Crusader remains, **Atlit** is among the best preserved. Were it not for the depredations of intervening generations, the "Castle of the Pilgrims" might have come down to us in its original form, because unlike the other Crusader strongholds throughout the country it was never destroyed in war, having been abandoned by the Crusaders in 1291. Unfortunately the castle, fort, and cathedral were dismantled over the centuries in order to build breakwaters, walls, and fortifications elsewhere. Parts of the cathedral remain, however, and you can see the outlines, parts of walls and towers, of the castle itself. To visit the site, you must first obtain a permit from the Government Tourist Information Office, 2 Balfour Street, Haifa. From the Castle of the Pilgrims you get a view of modern Israel at work at the *salt works* a mile down the coast. The production from Atlit not only fills the saltcellars of Israel but also is exported—much of it going to Africa.

From the Atlit crossroad to Haifa is another 10 miles, and en route you pass beaches and the site of the country's largest immigrant intake camp, *Sha'ar Aliya,* through which tens of thousands of newcomers have passed to permanent accommodation and settlement after a short stay. Nearing the port city, which rises from the sea up the slopes of the Carmel mountain, the highway is divided along the center by an attractive procession of stately palms and gay exotic blooms.

HAIFA: GATEWAY TO ISRAEL

The comparison that "Haifa is like our San Francisco," often made by generous Americans, or the opposite by homesick Israelis, has like all exaggeration enough of the truth. Carmel, the beautiful mount, descends to the sea—Haifa, the beautiful city, climbs the Carmel. Few ports, on first sight from the ocean, have brought so many lumps to the throat of man. To an entire people moving home in ships, Haifa is the gateway to Zion. Porters and customs officials at its docks have become hardened to the sight of immigrants and visitors who kneel to kiss its soil, weep, or dance. This is a place where parents and children, brothers and friends, long torn asunder by the world's turbulence and borders, end a very personal as well as national exile.

This, then, is Israel's main port, far more than the usual parade of sheds, cranes and ships, the litter of cargo, the masthead flags of many nations. Through its docks have poured most of Israel's million immigrants of the last 20 years. On the docks of Haifa you will see immigrants coming from Morocco clutching not suitcases but ragged bundles, piled-up crates of oranges for export, derricks swinging in caterpillar tractors and crated machines. To one side, in their own parts of the harbor, are the sleek gray warships and the stubby, untidy little fishing boats, and as you exit or enter the port gates you will see the press of people anxiously awaiting the arrival of new ships.

The beginnings of this second largest town in Israel (population about 200,000) are not known. Its name first appears in Talmudic literature at about the 3rd century A.D., but this entire coastline around the bay and the Zebulun Valley hinterland have been alive and throbbing since the Phoenicians. Incidentally, models of ancient Phoenician and Judaean sailing and merchant ships, once built in the days of Hyram of Tyre and King Solomon of wood from the heights of Carmel and Lebanon, are displayed at the *Maritime Museum,* near the port.

As to history, many and various are the suggestions about the origin of the name Haifa. Most popular, in mythology and guide books, are two claims. One is that the Hebrew words "Hof Yafeh" —beautiful coast—contracted some time in history to form the one word Haifa. The other is based on Caiaphas, High Priest of Jerusalem in the 1st century, believed to be the original city founder.

There are large gaps in the known history of the town but by the 3rd century Haifa's population was a mixture of Jewish inhabitants and Greek traders and shippers. Records exist of a valiant defense by Arabs and Jews who lived there during the Middle Ages when the Crusaders launched their seaborne invasion of 1100 A.D. When the Turks subsequently took over, its fortunes waned and Haifa's return to history only began anew when the Zionist immigrants at the end of the last century started to land at the port and resettle its immediate and hilly hinterland.

As with all ports, the first streets and thoroughfares of the modern town are near and parallel to the harbor. They mostly developed, as did the present port facilities, during the early days of the British Mandate. England, after all, was not slow to realize the strategic value of a naval base at the eastern end of the Mediterranean. Although now called *Independence Road,* old-timers still think of the main artery and business center near the harbor by its earlier name of "Kings Way."

Down at this level of the city are other relics of the British occupation. Near the Railway Station, from which the brand new diesel trains roar south to Tel Aviv and Jerusalem, is Plumer's Square, called after a British High Commissioner. Here are held Haifa's most colorful Independence Day celebrations when thousands of pioneer farmers, their wives and children, stream in from the nearby valleys to watch Circassians and Druzes do wild and traditional sword dances, competing in dash and virility.

Although Independence Road itself is a broad and imposing thoroughfare, replete with most modern banks, shops and office buildings, its side and parallel streets bear the unmistakable color and squalor of an until recently Arab residence. Some of the Arabs who decided to remain as Israel's citizens still live here as proprietors of the many "Oriental" cafés selling peeta, shishkebab and other delicacies, or from small hole-in-the-wall shops display their wares. There is also here some of the typical "bazaar" atmosphere of the east where the bargain-hunting visitor may be quick to respond.

Haifa harbor from high on Mount Carmel

The lower town, as most Israelis call the port section, has the usual nautical lure and lore. Sailors from a score of lands spend much of their leave and pay in its dives. Tourists are forever filling launches to "See Haifa and Akko from the Bay." At the feet of the Carmel, and to north, south and east, the lower town spreads with the seashore.

Haifa has, nevertheless, a perpendicular dimension which in fact constitutes the major portion of its spread. From the lower town to *Hadar HaCarmel,* the central section of the town, climb a maze of hairpin roads which, with each foot of elevation, present a permanent invitation for the land-or-sea-scape photographer. For the driver, the ascent is a challenge to the engine, the descent a test for brakes. If you wish to avoid both there is now the brand new subway, from harbor to mountain top, or from zero to a thousand feet above sea level. In honor of its French builders, the square on which the lowest station is located has been named "Paris."

Approaching it from the sea, Hadar circles the center of the Carmel as a blazing girdle of light. Its story, expressed by the strictly functional character of most of its square, angular apartment houses and buildings, is largely that of the immigrants from Germany of the mid-1930's. Many of them, still by that date, could bring the wherewithal out of Hitlerland to build their own houses and stores on the Carmel's slopes. Their whiteness gives to Haifa that cleaned, scrubbed and orderly look which singles it out along the entire Mediterranean. The most elaborate and prosperous of these houses, not to mention some of the city's best hotels, are sited further up, above Hadar, the loftiest climbing to the highest plateau of the hill.

The contribution of German immigrants apart, Haifa's essential personality was formed and maintained by its earliest settlers from eastern Europe. This is best symbolized by the city's late mayor, Abba Khushi, a dynamic, forceful and patriarchal type who successfully imposed his will in many directions. Backed by his distinctly labor municipality and council, Khushi has seen to it that Haifa runs its bus service on the Sabbath, the city's wealthier citizens pay a large percentage of the taxes (they claim too large), and the old-age pensioners have annual tours around the country and other amenities. The city's accent upon parks and gardens, and its palm– and flower–lined entrance are among his innovations.

To the visitor, the three major ingredients of Haifa—labor, religion and learning—will become immediately apparent. Many of the largest industrial enterprises in its environs are trade union owned and managed. They include such factories as Nesher Cement, Vulcan Foundry, Phoenicia Glass, the large steel mills on the road to Akko, and the new shipyards. Together with the chain of cooperative-type villages encircling Haifa, they give that city much of its flavor. Private endeavor, however, has not been inhibited by this as the large oil refineries and Chemicals and Fertilizers Limited testify.

The city's religious sites make interesting tourist fare. They range from the magnificent Bahai Temple and exquisite gardens to the Cave of Elijah; they include impressive monasteries and shrines. Some are as old as the Canaanite and Philistine periods, as can be expected from a mountain, both refuge and sanctuary to nearly every cult and faith practiced in this holy land. It is the *Bahai Temple* that really catches eye and breath. To the rail of an approaching ship or to most of the Carmel beckons the gold of its plated dome.

Buried in the Temple is Mirza Ali Mohammed, forerunner of this unique faith which seeks to unite all religions into one spiritual confederation under the One God, with Moses, Christ, Mohammed and Buddha as coequal prophets. As the Haifa Temple is the world center, the faith's archives and museum adjoin it in a Parthenon-type building. (The Bahai founder, Baha–Ulla, is interred near Akko, also amid delightful gardens.)

As to *Elijah's Cave*, it is not below the *Carmelite Monastery*, although it is to the Carmelite Order that this prophet is patron saint. There is a cave associated with Elijah (and Elisha his disciple) beneath the impressive Carmelite building and hence its holiness. The actual Cave, in which the Prophet sheltered and hid from the King of Israel, is two miles away, at the foot of Carmel and is sacred to the Jewish population. If, after a congested program of travel and tour, you find in yourself symptoms of nervous disorder, a few days in Elijah's grotto habitat will, according to tradition, set you right again.

While on the subject of caves, it is worth mentioning that to archaeologists the most famous are those of *Et-Tabun* at the foot of the Carmel, near Haifa. It was here that the British Garrod expedition of the 1930's discovered the skeletons and artifacts of Homo palestinensis, the last link in the anthropological chain

The dome of the Bahai Temple shines in the Mediterranean sun

between Neanderthal and present-day man. These skeletons and various primitive flint tools found with them are at least 100,000 years old.

Haifa's prize edifice of learning, however, deals neither with archaeology nor anthropology, but with nuclear physics, electronics, various types of engineering, aerodynamics and architecture. It is the *Israel Institute of Technology,* the "Technion" in popular language, and often known as the country's M.I.T. The early, and still-used, campus is in Hadar HaCarmel but a striking, ultra-modern complex now enhances the north-eastern slopes of the mount. One can only envy the students already studying and living at this new site. It commands a breathtaking view, beautiful grounds and a series of highly original, yet tastefully designed structures.

One of the highlights, featuring "night-life" during Haifa's summer are the public symphony concerts in the *Mothers' Garden.* Citizens of all ages flock to them with their rugs and blankets and spread out, informally, on the lawns. The number of young people, and the intensity of their interest, are most unusual. The streams, glens and rock shrubbery which cover this park make it an attractive picnic site.

Also worth viewing are Haifa's handsome municipal buildings, the new city theater, the landscaping around the *Law Courts,* the museums—ethnic, archaeological and of modern art—and the illuminations from the upper reaches of the town which challenge any imagined Disney fairyland. And, of course, by sunny day, the beaches are as good as any and a few minutes' ride from the lower town.

NORTHERN
COASTAL PLAIN
WESTERN
GALILEE

From Haifa to the Lebanese border at Rosh Hanikra is less than 26 miles. Between these two points, following the Mediterranean shore, lie Akko (Acre), one of the world's most ancient cities, Shavei Zion, Nahariya, and the villages of the Zebulun plain.

Depending upon the amount of time you wish to spend in one or each of these places, you can decide whether to extend this trip by visiting Montfort and Peki'in as well. All can be done without much strain in a day, and you can still return to Haifa in the evening and rest or plan a late program there.

Akko (Acre). The 14-mile journey to this famous port is through the Haifa industrial belt and large residental suburbs called *kiryot*. The kibbutz village on the right before you reach the bridge over the Na'aman River (Belus of the Greeks) is *Kfar Masaryk,* named after Czechoslovakia's first democratic president. .Almost next door, cultivating the same rich black soil of the valley, its economy enhanced by artificial carp ponds, is the kibbutz *Ein Hamifratz.* A little more than a mile past the Na'aman Bridge is a traffic circle from which one road leads westwards to the Old Town of Akko and a second, on the right, to the New Town.

The name of Akko appears in written history as far back as 1500 B.C. in the records of the Pharaoh Thutmose III of Egypt. A prime natural port, it has a history that is turbulent even for this turbulent land. Akko has flourished throughout most of its history. A part of the land of the tribe of Asher, it was subsequently ruled by the Egyptians, Assyrians, Persians, Romans, Greeks, and Moslems. It was the capital of the Crusaders' eastern empire after the fall of Jerusalem, and fell into disuse and neglect under the Turks. Revived and fortified in the 18th century by Ahmad el Jazzar, "the Butcher" and his predecessor (whom he murdered) Daher el Omar, it withstood the assaults of Napoleon during his ill-fated attempts to make Palestine a French satellite. He was turned back at Akko by the combined defense led by el Jazzar and the British fleet under Sir Sidney Smith—a defeat which ended his dreams of Asian conquest.

Pliny (23–79 A.D.) credits Akko as the site of the accidental discovery of glass. According to this prolific gentleman, Phoenician sailors landing at the mouth of the Na'aman River heated blocks of niter which, mixed with the fine sand of the river banks, hardened into the substance we now know as glass.

The *Old Town* of Akko is perhaps the most oriental in aspect in Israel since most of what you see today was built by el Jazzar at the end of the 18th century. Near the harbor starts the *ancient market* which occupies almost all of the Old Town. Its streets are cobbled, twisted, and narrow, most of its shops little more than recessed dingy stalls. It is a labyrinth, always crowded, and you can buy practically anything here from drums to food. Sitting on chairs outside tiny cafés are the old men smoking their hooka pipes, the long stems of which pass through water to cool the smoke. In the market Arabs in traditional costume and immigrants from the new section of the town mix freely. It is useful to single out landmarks for your return course out of the market, as all of its streets and buildings are deceptively alike to the inexperienced eye.

The Citadel, which is just inside the ancient wall separating the Old Town from the New, rose during el Jazzar's era and played many rôles in the life of the city. It was Jazzar's treasury, and later, during the British Mandate, a prison. After World War II and before Israel's independence, Akko's Citadel held hundreds of Jewish political prisoners. Today it is a mental hospital. If you have read the book or seen the film *Exodus,* you will find it a familiar sight. Although a comparative newcomer as far as buildings go in Israel, the Citadel was built on the foundations of a much earlier fortification erected by the Crusaders.

The *Jazzar Mosque* nearer the center of the Old Town and facing a large square is also a relic of the notorious pasha. To the right of this impressive building is Jazzar's tomb in a separate building. A few hundred feet further to the right, and down a small street, is the *Hammam el Basha* which houses the municipal museum. If you continue through Akko's winding streets, you will come to the *Church of St. George,* Greek-Orthodox and the oldest of the several Christian churches in Old Akko, and further along, near the sea, *St. Andrew's Church.*

On the other side (Haifa side) of the Old Town, near the little harbor are several large *caravanserai* where warehouse facilities for the goods brought in by camel train and accommodations for the drivers and merchants were provided. The caravan trade, for which Akko was one of the main ports, flourished until comparatively recent times.

The *New Town,* which has surrounded and dwarfed Old Akko, is an ever-growing mass of immigrants' houses. Their architecture is strictly functional, and they have the usual square white and raw look, often colored by washing hanging from a line or balcony. The city has a population of 33,000—as opposed to fewer than 10,000 before independence. It is predominantly Jewish, although there are still modest Christian and Moslem communities in the Old Town.

A little more than a mile north through the fertile Akko plain is the *Bahai Shrine,* the tomb of Baha-Ulla, and the sect's museum which includes some very fine paintings and rugs. A little further on you see a high *aqueduct* parallel to the road. Don't let anyone tell you it's Roman—it was built at the end of the 18th century to bring water to Akko. In the kibbutz village *Lohamei Hagetaot* —Ghetto Fighters—started in 1949 by Jewish partisans on the anniversary of the Warsaw Ghetto uprising, you will find the *Beit Katznelson Museum* which is dedicated to preserving the records of the Nazi death camps and the eastern European ghettos of World War II.

Less than two miles before you reach Nahariya, a signpost to the left side of the road points seawards and reads *Shavei Zion.* This seaside resort village was founded in the late thirties by Jewish refugees from southern Germany. The famous *Dolphin House* is a resort hotel, and if you have spent the morning in Akko, you might do well to stop here for lunch on your way north or east.

Nahariya was also founded by German settlers in 1934. Its main income is drawn from a beautiful beach and summer boarding houses, always full in season, although lying as it does in the fertile plain of Akko, it is also a hard-working farming community. A Canaanite temple was discovered near the beach here in 1947, and in the vicinity you can find the remains of burial grounds belonging to several bygone civilizations.

By this time you are only 5 miles south of the Lebanese-Israel border, guarded by an outpost on a white cliff called *Rosh Hanikra,* which juts out into the sea. Before you reach this lovely piece of scenery, the road passes the American-sabra kibbutz, *Gesher Haziv,* and the ruins of *Akhziv,* a town of the tribe of Asher where some years ago archaeologists found a number of unopened tombs. Here too is the French recreation village run by the famous Club Mediterranée. Another village around here is called *Liman* to honor Senator Herbert H. Lehman. Rosh Hanikra, the frontier outpost between Israel and Lebanon, sits on a high promontory over the sea. From the uppermost parts you can look down the coast to Akko and Haifa and westward over the Mediterranean. Down below, at sea level, the grotto in the chalk cliffs can vie with that of Capri. A cable car runs from the cafe at the top of the cliff to the grottos below, where the view can be enjoyed in dry comfort from behind glass screens. As the road goes no further in Israel, you may wish to turn eastwards in the direction of Montfort, Yehiam, and Peki'in before returning to Haifa.

From Nahariya to Peki'in is about 14 miles, and between them lie such historic sites as the Crusaders' fort of Judin; the settlement of Yehiam; Montfort, the castle of the Teutonic knights; and the village of Me'ona. Of the plentiful Crusader ruins in this entire area, **Montfort** is probably the best known. It crests a precipitous hillside, and is surrounded by higher mountains. The

The seas off Haifa yield a generous catch

road to the castle peters out a little more than a mile before you get to the entrance, and from here you follow a foot path. It is easy to see why Montfort, or Starkburg as it was called by the Teutonic knights, held out as long as it did at the end of the Crusader period. The only entrance is the path you now take. On the other three sides there are walls which are all but unscalable. Here the German knights held out against Saracen attacks for five years before a negotiated peace was made with Beibars. Although only sections of walls remain, the outline of the fort is still clearly visible. A major excavation job was done by an American expedition in 1926, and Crusader relics they collected can be seen at the Metropolitan Museum in New York and the Rockefeller Museum in the Old City of Jerusalem.

The most interesting of all the sights of this area to Israelis is the village of **Old Peki'in.** Primarily a community of Christians and Druzes, it is noteworthy as the place where Jews have lived without interruption since the time of the Second Temple.

Near the old village is a modern Jewish settlement called *New Peki'in*. Before you set out for this limited area, within a 15-mile radius of Nahariya, take with you a detailed map, for the sites here are so close to each other it is easy to miss some of them.

THE
JEZREEL VALLEY
AND
LOWER GALILEE

Around Haifa, within a radius of 20 miles, are many of the country's most interesting archaeological and historic sites. Some of them are on the way to regions such as the Jezreel Valley and Lower Galilee, but it is better to dedicate a day or half days to these sites in the more immediate Haifa region so that the extensive touring into the north will not be crowded.

A visit to Beit She'arim, on one of the main routes into the Jezreel Valley, is a case in point. Its excavations are among the most extensive that have been made and some of the places en route, Yagur, Sha'ar Ha'amakim, Kiryat Amal, or Tivon are worth visiting.

BEIT SHE'ARIM, MEGIDDO AND DALIYAT EL KARMIL

The 11-mile route to Beit She'arim from Haifa passes the huge *Nesher Cement Factory,* one of the largest enterprises of the labor federation Histadrut. Its profits, by the way, go back into the Histadrut treasury for new and further pioneer investment, mostly, these days, in the Negev south. Not far down the road is the kibbutz village of *Yagur,* veteran pioneer settlement with an interesting museum of finds made in the area, and near it, on a rise overlooking the road, *Sha'ar Ha'amikim*—Gate of the Valleys—so called because it stands on the threshold of Zebulun to the north and Jezreel to the south.

The two villages, Yagur and Sha'ar Ha'amakim, provide an interesting contrast, even though both are of the kibbutz type. Each is the product of a separate movement with different concepts of how to build this form of village. The Sha'ar Ha'amakim people, for example, started with the idea of a tiny agricultural community of 20 or 30 families, small enough, they claimed, to maintain the intimacy and brotherhood of a family and provide thereby greatest possibilities for individual expression and values. The Yagur people, on the other hand, had the idea at the beginning that the entire country could be built as one huge kibbutz and that their own village should be unlimited in the size of its membership and growth. The small village, they said, would stifle the human and cultural milieu of the individual, produce parochialism, and be restricted in its economic possibilities as well. How these two contrasting theories have worked out in the years of growth of these two villages may be an interesting incentive to visit them.

The road leads into the southernmost Galilean hills, beautifully forested, gentle, richly green. You pass the resort of *Tivon,* and on a hill nearby find the internationally famous youth intake center of *Ramat Hadassah,* named in honor of Henrietta Szold, the wonderful American woman who has become almost a legend in modern Israel. Her entire life was dedicated to building the Youth Aliya organization, the support of which is one of American Hadassah's main preoccupations. Since it began its work in 1933 in Germany with the rescue of children orphaned by the Nazi regime and their pioneer education and training in Israel, over 100,000 youngsters from 13 to 17 have been its graduates. Ramat Hadassah, a maze of educational facilities and habitation, is where these youths, now mostly from North African and Eastern European countries, receive initial training and build the groups which then go out with their Youth Aliya instructors to pioneer villages, or to the various specialized schools and vocational centers of Youth Aliya throughout the country. Many of these groups have subsequently established their own new pioneer villages on completing training in the veteran settlements.

Restoration of the ruins at Beit She'arim

The ruins of **Beit She'arim** are on lower ground to the right of the main highway. An ancient Jewish city, Beit She'arim was the seat of the *Sanhedrin* or Supreme Court in the 2nd and 3rd centuries A.D. after the destruction of the Second Temple. The remains of the city which had been lying forgotten since some time in the 4th century, were unearthed by a scientific expedition about 25 years ago. You can see the ruins of a large synagogue, and a short way away, extensive catacombs in which the distinguished dead of Beit She'arim were buried.

From Beit She'arim return along the main highway to about a mile before Yagur where a road branching leftwards is the western gateway to the Jezreel Valley. Along this road some 5 or 6 miles we come to the kibbutz village of **Hazorea,** often in the news because of the exhibitions of local antiquities as well as contemporary art. Its museum, the *Wilfrid Israel House,* also boasts a unique oriental art collection which was bequeathed to Hazorea by Wilfrid Israel who was a victim of the same plane crash that ended the life of Leslie Howard. Hazorea is also famous for its public performances of various folk operas presented throughout the country by its very creative and talented inhabitants. Its immediate neighbor is **Mishmar HaEmek—** Guardian of the Valley—one of the oldest of Israel's pioneer villages, established in 1927. The high school here is one of the best in the country, and many young people from the cities have been sent here for study. During the 1948 war, Mishmar HaEmek heroically repelled the attack of a large army commanded by the soldier of fortune Kaukji, and its resistance was one of the turning points leading to the defeat of the Arab invasion.

Over 2 miles from Mishmar HaEmek (17 miles from Haifa) you reach the foot of the Samarian mountains and the ruins of one of the oldest and most famous cities of ancient times, Megiddo.

To Israelis, the name **Megiddo** is connected with the power, opulence, and wisdom of King Solomon. But its history is far older than that. King Thutmose III of Egypt took Megiddo in

1478 B.C., and the test samplings of archaeologists show evidence that there have been at least 20 different cities on this single site. For certain Egyptian, Canaanite, Israelite, and Assyrian cultures have built here over the centuries; and perhaps many more. The reasons for this long history of building and destruction can be found in Megiddo's strategic position between the Jordan Valley and the sea, and on the route between Egypt and Mesopotamia.

The Bible tells us that after Deborah defeated King Jabin of the Canaanites, the Israelites took Megiddo. Later in the First Book of Kings it is written that Solomon fortified the city: "And this is the reason of the levy which King Solomon raised; for to build the house of the Lord, and his own house, and Millo, and the wall of Jerusalem, and Hazor, and Megiddo, and Gezer." And later in the Second Book of Chronicles: "And Solomon had four thousand stalls for horses and chariots, and twelve thousand horsemen; whom he bestowed in the chariot cities, and with the king at Jerusalem."

The excavations at Megiddo which began in the nineteen twenties under the auspices of the University of Chicago and are still underway, have uncovered the remains of an enormous double entrance gate from the time of Solomon—and his oft-boasted *stables*. These stables—each housing up to 120 horses, were long rectangular buildings, each with an aisle down the center and stalls on either side. The stalls were divided by stone columns to which

Horseback riding on the Mediterranean shore of Atlit

the horses were chained. The roofs to these stables, of course, have long since disappeared, but they have been restored so that you can see where the rows of columns stood with mangers in between. Also brought to light by the archaeologists is a large building thought to have been a palace. In the eastern part of the mound near the stables are the remains of a *Canaanite temple* of around 1900 B.C., containing two altars. Many of the Megiddo finds, including one of the altars from the Canaanite temple, can be seen at the Oriental Institute of the University of Chicago.

From Megiddo you can either return to Haifa the way you came, or turn left at the Elyakim crossroads to reenter the city through the Ahuza suburb. This route will take you through the Druze villages of Daliyat el Karmil and Isfiya. This route is a little longer than the other, but it is also more beautiful, winding, as it does, up the inland slopes of the Carmel.

Like all of the Druze villages in western Galilee, **Daliyat el Karmil** caps a height amid the mountains. At first glance the village of stone cut from the hills will appear to you like any other Arab hamlet in the country. It is true the menfolk wear the dashing headdress, the *kaffiya,* and long striped robe, and the women are discreetly hidden from male view. The Druzes are nevertheless insistent upon their differences from the Arabs, not only in matters of religion, but in tradition and custom as well. Unlike the Moslem faith, in which no demand is made on the womenfolk to pray, Druze services only begin when there is an equal number of women and men in the mosque, for Druze souls are equal. A warrior people, brave and vital, they trace, although cannot prove, their ancestry to Aro-Indian stock, and all consider themselves related to the Druze people of the Syrian mountains. Most of the inhabitants of Daliyat el Karmil are Druzes, but the village also contains some Christians. *Isfiya,* over 2 miles away, is another mixed village of Druzes and Christians.

Isfiya, Daliyat el Karmil, and other Druze villages of the Carmel feature tobacco growing as the mainstay of their economy which also consists of olive plantations and horticulture. Most of them have already been linked up with main highways by new approach roads, and more and more now have electricity and running water. From Isfiya back to Haifa is just another few miles.

AFULA, EIN HAROD, BEIT SHA'AN AND THE JORDAN VALLEY

Another day excursion in the area of the Jezreel Valley takes you out through the fast-growing market town of **Afula,** about 28 miles from Haifa. The town is the distribution center for many of the crops grown in the lush Jezreel Valley and is the home of a number of plants engaged in light manufacture. Though little of its past is evident—the base of an ancient Arab tower built on an

Communal dining hall of a kibbutz

even older burial mound can be seen in the southern portion of
the town—Afula has had a long and interesting history. It is the
site of still another Crusader stronghold, and also of one of
Napoleon's victories during his adventure in the Holy Land. The
present day town was pioneered in 1925, and has grown up
considerably in the last few years.

Continuing along the road from Haifa through Afula you pass
a number of busy farming communities such as *Kfar Yehezkel*
and *Geva*. Some six miles past the market city you come to a
turnoff to the left of the road leading to **Ein Harod,** a kibbutz
settled forty years ago by pioneers from Russia. It is a large

community of diversified industries—well known as an intellectual and artistic center.

Less than a mile past the Ein Harod junction a road to the right leads you toward two of Israel's most interesting archaeological finds—Beit Alfa and Beit Sha'an. Here at the foot of Mount Gilboa pioneers draining the swampland unearthed the remains of a large synagogue at **Beit Alfa** of the 6th century A.D. and with it a remarkably handsome *mosaic floor*. Embroidered around the edges with decorative characters and inscribed at the bottom with the names of the designers, the mosaic is divided into three panels. The first shows Abraham preparing the sacrifice of Isaac. The style is primitive and direct, and although the scene is completely clear, the main characters are labeled to insure identification. The central panel is a zodiacal wheel covering almost half the area of the entire floor. The last and upper panel contains a number of religious symbols: the Ark, menorah, shofar, two lions and a curtain. The effect is symmetrical while not being completely rigid. If you have the time, a half hour's visit to Beit Alfa's synagogue is well worthwhile.

The main goal of this trip is less than five miles down the road from Beit Alfa—the village and archaeological mound of Beit Sha'an.

Strategically situated as it is at the entrance from the valley of the Jordan River to the Jezreel Valley, **Beit Sha'an** is a city whose history reaches far back to the beginning of the era of records. Allotted to the tribe of Menasseh by Joshua, it had earlier been a major Canaanite city dedicated to the snake god Shakan. King Saul was killed at Mount Gilboa nearby in a battle with the Philistines, and his body and those of his sons were hung outside the city walls. The city was finally reduced by Solomon and it became one of his main defense posts and commissary headquarters. The Romans took the city in 63 B.C. and the Arabs destroyed it in the 7th century A.D.

Despite its record of destruction and conquest Beit Sha'an because of its location in an enormously rich, food-producing area, has never been completely abandoned. There have been Jewish communities here off and on throughout the years; the last one having been in the nineteen thirties. The present town was founded in 1949.

Excavations of the great mound which rises to the east of the town shows evidences of civilizations almost back as far as those of Megiddo. Artifacts from the Egyptian period were uncovered by an expedition digging under the auspices of the University of Pennsylvania (1921–23), as well as successive cities, layer on layer, which showed that Beit Sha'an had been the site of Israelite, Philistine, Assyrian, and Byzantine cultures. Much of the

Olive tree in Galilee

archaeological treasure found here is in the Rockefeller Museum in Jerusalem's Old City. It includes Egyptian sarcophagi and jewels, ancient plaques with inscriptions in Hebrew, Egyptian steles of Seti I and Ramses II, and many other prizes of incalculable value. Some of the artifacts were brought back by the expedition and can be seen in the University's museum; others are in a small museum at Beit Sha'an.

Not far away from the mound is a *Roman theater* in remarkably good condition, the best preserved in Israel.

If your interest in the past is strong, Beit Sha'an should take a good deal of your time. If, however, you are more concerned with the Israel of today, you will want to continue through the central Jordan Valley for which Beit Sha'an is the key, and north to the Sea of Galilee.

On the road to Degania, which sits at the southern end of the Sea of Galilee, you pass a number of moshavot and kibbutzim established here to take advantage of the rich soil of the Jordan Valley. *Beit Yosef* is 6 miles from Beit Sha'an. This moshav was settled in the late 1930's and is named for Yosef Aharonowitz, a pioneer in the settlement of Israel.

Before you get to Gesher, the next town of any size along this road, you pass the Crusader fort of *Belvoir. Gesher,* at the confluence of the Yarmuk and the Jordan, was founded in 1939 by German pioneers.

Between Gesher and Degania are half a dozen other small settlements, all agricultural, flanking the road as it drops down toward the lake. From Degania, described later, you can either return to Haifa over one of a number of routes, or you can go on to Tiberias another 6 miles along the lake shore, spend the night in one of its several good hotels and continue your Galilean journeys the following day.

TO LOWER GALILEE

The following itinerary has no pretensions of touring all of Lower Galilee, but instead is designed to get you to most—not all—of the interesting sites en route. You can cover it all in one day—it's only a little more than 100 miles altogether—but if you did so, you would be doing yourself a disservice. A much better plan would be to break the trip overnight at Tiberias or Safed (Safed in summer, Tiberias in winter).

The first main stop on the way to Nazareth from Haifa is the first *moshav oudim,* smallholders' village, Nahalal, in the western sector of the Jezreel Valley. From Haifa to Nahalal is 19 miles, flashing past Beit She'arim en route, and from the Nahalal crossroads to Nazareth another 8. From Nazareth to Tiberias through Kfar Kana is a further 20. In other words, a total journey of less than 50 miles brings you to a small part of the western Jezreel Valley into Lower Galilee, leaving adequate time—including the return journey—to cover the latter area and to get back to Haifa the same evening.

As you drive along the highway to **Nahalal** and drop to the Valley of Jezreel, a beautiful, flat, fertile plain, it is difficult to believe that less than four decades ago this was the treacherous malarial swamp, called in Arabic the "Valley of Death." It is a checkerboard of green crops and the rich brown of the ploughed fields, speckled and bordered by the groups of white villages as far as the eye can see. Among the earliest of these settlements was Nahalal, the most photographed *moshav*—cooperative small-holders' settlement. Aerial pictures show it as a wide circle with the white houses around its perimeter and the farmsteads and central buildings, groves of trees and pathways leading inwards to a central hub. Americans will immediately be struck by the thought that this is a closed circular stockade, much like their own frontier settlements in the early days of the American West, built in a form to protect the inhabitants and their possessions from marauders.

The fact is that when the first settlers of Nahalal moved into the swamp, they were in dire need of such protection. As they reclaimed the land, grew crops, acquired livestock and gave birth to children, they were under frequent attack by pillaging nomads and for years, until at last internal peace came to the Valley, the defense perimeter kept it secure.

Nahalal's settlers were originally members of the first kibbutz, Degania, on the shores of the Sea of Galilee. They left it to form their own village because they felt cooperative, rather than collective, farming satisfied more the craving for individual expression. They decided on family farmsteads and kept the kibbutz principle of self-labor. Only the farmer and his family worked their land, no hired help was permitted. Degania's principles of mutual aid were worked out in Nahalal in a different way. Communally owned property became limited to the central institutions, the heavy machinery and main irrigation system of the village. This was paid for through equitable self–taxation. Orange groves, to which each family gave equal amounts of labor and withdrew equal profits, were also a community undertaking. Work and profits on the family farm, however, were a private affair. A system of cooperative purchasing and marketing of products evolved as this proved to be more economical and efficient than individual efforts by the separate farmers. When sickness, military service or other extraordinary occurrences prevented an individual farmer from working his land, all the other farmers worked it for him.

Nahalal merits a visit not only as it is the first, oldest and most developed of Israel's chain of moshav villages—the predominant form of rural settlement in the country—but also because its earliest members in particular are interesting people. You can see here three generations living side by side and feel the atmosphere of a peasantry with a tradition and not one in the process of self-manufacture, as is the case in many of the newest villages.

Entrance to Nahalal is through a pleasant eucalyptus avenue and flanked by the WIZO Agricultural School. In the hub of this circle are school buildings, synagogue, community center, and memorial monument to the sons of Nahalal who fell in the 1948 war. It bears the inscription: "From the silence of the stone we call—Remember!" According to the Bible, the sons of the tribe of Zebulun inherited this valley and Nahalal was one of their towns.

The highway eastwards from Nahalal climbs into the hills of Galilee and the Jezreel Valley drops behind. The road coils across a flat highland as it passes the *Balfour Forest* on the mountain slopes to the right. Still climbing, you pass the Christian-Arab village of *Yafi'a,* a Judaean redoubt in the revolt against the Romans. From Yafi'a you can see the stone and white buildings of **Nazareth,** the city of Jesus, nestling in the heart of the mountains. Until recently the city was completely populated by Christians and Moslems, but in 1957 a new suburb called Kiryat Natzrat was added to accommodate Jewish immigrants from Eastern Europe.

Although apparently it had been in existence for several centuries before the Christian Era, Nazareth was not of great enough significance to have been mentioned in the Bible. The little hill town was a quiet hamlet inhabited by sheepherders and farmers out of the direct course of history which teemed through the

Nazareth from the roof of the Church of the Annunciation

Jezreel Valley a few miles to the south. It became a ,
importance, of course, through its association with Jesus. Josepᵣ
and Mary were both citizens of the town, and it was here that the
Angel of the Lord appeared before Mary and told her of the
forthcoming birth of Jesus. Nazareth is also the town in which
Jesus grew up; it was at the synagogue here he studied and
learned; and here he preached in the temple and was proclaimed
the Messiah. Angered by what they felt was blaspheming, the
citizens of Nazareth turned on him and drove him from the town.
There is no record that Jesus ever returned to the scene of his
boyhood, but it has been revered ever afterward by Christians,
and during the Crusades was one of the main goals of the
conquest of the Holy Land.

Records which have come down to us indicate that Nazareth
remained a Jewish town until the Crusades, although there is
evidence that a Christian church was built here some 500 years
earlier. During the hundred and fifty years or so that the western
knights held sway in the land, the town changed hands several
times, being finally destroyed by Beibars in the last half of the
13th century. While they held Nazareth, the Crusaders had built
several churches, on the ruins of one of which the present day
Church of the Annunciation was built.

The town began to take on its present character during the
time of the Turk Daher who tolerated the return of Christians,
both Arab and Western.

Regrettably, this spiritual center, so important to all of
Christianity is not entirely free of the Levantine atmosphere of
"baksheesh" and commercialism. Despite government efforts to
reduce this unfortunate impression by fixing rates for tours and
providing accredited guides, enough local amateurs of all ages
persistently offer their services and are a nuisance. Nor do the
various rival claims of churches that theirs are the only possible
authentic sites connected with the life of Joseph, Mary, and Jesus
enhance the over-all dignity the place deserves. Nevertheless,
there is enough of the authentic to inspire and humble, and
sufficient to overcome these disabilities.

The recently completed *Church of the Annunciation,* belonging to the Franciscans, is built on the ruins of a Crusader church,
over the grotto in which the Virgin Mary was visited by the
Angel. In the first chapter of the Gospel of St. Luke in the
New Testament it is recorded: "And in the sixth month the angel
Gabriel was sent from God unto a city of Galilee, named
Nazareth, to a virgin espoused to a man whose name was Joseph,
of the house of David; and the virgin's name was Mary. And the
angel came in unto her, and said, Hail thou art highly favored,
and the Lord is with thee: blessed art thou among women . . .

And, behold, thou shalt conceive in thy womb and bring forth a son, and shalt call His name Jesus. He shall be great, and shall be called the Son of the Highest . . ."

The grotto, which can be visited, has in it two pillars, one thought to be in the place where the angel Gabriel stood, and the other at the point where Mary was when he appeared. Also in the caves below the church is a place designated as the tomb of Joseph.

Nearby is the *Church of St. Joseph,* also a Franciscan church which is said to have been built on the site of the house in which Jesus, Mary, and Joseph lived. On the road toward Tiberias is another church, *St. Gabriel,* which claims the same distinction. Close to the Church of St. Gabriel is the *Fountain of the Virgin* where you can see the village well to which Mary went daily for water.

Other important Christian shrines and holy places in Nazareth are the *synagogue* in which Jesus studied and later preached, and the *precipice* where it is said the enraged townspeople planned to throw Jesus over the edge of a cliff.

The town of Nazareth itself is of rare beauty, the view from its upper reaches is of mountain, precipice, and valley. The colorful market place contains the myriad of arched shops so characteristic of the Middle East. New industry is being brought to the town as it was inherited in 1948 with a shortage of work and water. The latter has been remedied, but the poverty is a longer job. Full employment will undoubtedly reduce much of the soliciting around the religious shrines which are dominantly Greek or Latinate Catholic. All sections of the Christian faith, however, are represented among the mainly Christian-Arab inhabitants of the town.

Some 4½ miles northeast of Nazareth on the road to Tiberias is another Christian holy place—*Kfar Kana,* the Cana of Galilee of the New Testament. It is here that Jesus performed his first miracle (John 2, 1-11) in which he changed water into wine. A church built in the 19th century on the ruins of several earlier houses of worship contains urns venerated as the water pots used in the miracle. There is also an older Greek Orthodox church in the town. Like Nazareth, Kfar Kana is a predominantly Christian community.

From Kfar Kana to Tiberias is about 15 miles on a road that winds through the gentle Galilean hills. A mile or two outside the city you reach a point where you can see the whole lake before you, surrounded by the rich plains of the Jordan Valley, and backed by the Syrian mountains. The lake itself is some 680 feet below sea level so the drop to the lakeside town is spectacular.

The beautiful sea, called Kinneret in Hebrew as it is shaped like a harp, has inspired some of Israel's poets to verse, and its artists to color. The hue of sun and mountain, at times so brilliant and sharp, is as elusive on canvas as the smile of the Mona Lisa.

Tiberias, with its great summer heat and large influx of newcomers, is understandably expanding upwards toward the mountaintop 1,200 feet above the lake. In winter the town is a pleasantly warm resort; in summer without shade it can be uncomfortable. A popular story is told about the connections between Tiberias, down at the lake, and Safed, on the top of the distant mountains. Both towns, it claims, live off each other; in the winter the inhabitants of Safed occupy Tiberias' guest houses—in summer the inhabitants of Tiberias return the compliment by having their holiday in Safed.

Herod Antipas, Tetrarch of Galilee and Perea and son of Herod the Great, established the city in the first quarter of the 1st century A.D. and made it his capital. A fortified city, it was named in honor of the Roman Emperor Tiberius. The Jews of the region refused to help in its building as its site was on the burial grounds of the ancient city of Rakkath, and it was considered unclean. Eventually, however, a Jewish population did grow up in Tiberias. During the Jewish uprising, Josephus, whose chronicle of the period is so valuable to scholars and historians, was in command of the Jewish legions which were based there. After the destruction of the Second Temple in Jerusalem, it became the center of Jewish learning. Toward the end of the 2nd century A.D. it became the seat of the Sanhedrin and of the Talmudic schools. It was in Tiberias that the Mishna was compiled and a century later the Gemara. The vowel system developed in order to prevent misreading and misinterpretation of the scriptures was also developed here. Maimonides, the great Talmudic scholar who is remembered also for his early concepts of medicine as a science is buried in Tiberias.

The Arabs occupied the city in the 7th century A.D. and in the

The Church of the Beatitudes on the shores of the Sea of Galilee

12th century it was a Crusader stronghold. Its fortunes rose and fell in succeeding centuries, and so did its walls and houses. Yet relics of the various eras of the city still stand today, others have been rebuilt, and of course there is much that is new, a modern city spreading out around the old.

Like so many cities in this ancient land, Tiberias is divided into an *old town,* built of the black basalt stone of the region, and a *new town* built in recent years outside the walls of the original city. The old town of Tiberias, down by the water's edge, is the place to look if you are interested in investigating the traces of the city's history. Here are the *tombs of Maimonides and Yohanan Ben Zakkai* as well as those of a number of the other Jewish thinkers whose home was here, the most important of which is that of *Rabbi Meir Ba'al Haness,* a mile or so south along the shore at the Hot Springs. You will find an *archaeological museum* in the old town, and in it collections of relics found in the area.

The curative powers of the water from the hot mineral springs found in the vicinity of Tiberias have been recognized for thousands of years—since before the time of Solomon. Herod Antipas, the city's founder, built baths here on the order of those near Rome. The pools he built, reconstructed again and again throughout the centuries can still be seen, and in the winter season the modern versions of these ancient baths are crowded with visitors who have come for their beneficial effects.

By the lakeside is the excellent *Galei Kinneret Hotel,* which counts among its regular visitors former Prime Minister Ben-Gurion.

The road to Degania, 5 miles away, passes the mineral baths and follows the lake shore.

Degania. In the year 1910 a group of 10 men and 2 women from the small Russian town of Romni settled on the swampy fringe of the Jordan Valley where the river empties into the Sea of Galilee. The place was then called Um Jima. Today, surrounded by orchards and gardens, by green fields of vegetables and corn wrested from the swamp, the village of Degania now stands as a showpiece of modern Israel. The group of 12 invented the kibbutz and served as an example to the hundred thousand people who now live in this type of village throughout the country. Everything Degania owns, whether housing, buildings, implements, or anything else, is shared and worked by and for the entire community. Profit is collective, it is shared equally by everyone as goods and services, the remaining reinvested to develop the farm. Everything is decided democratically and managed by elected committees. It has the community dining hall, typical of all such villages, children's houses where they live and learn, and an environment for adult habitation more like a park than a village. Beautiful trees, satin green lawns and exotic flowers shade and caress its white houses.

One of the highlights is Degania's agricultural and natural science museum, *Beit Gordon,* named after the philosopher and member A. D. Gordon who provided great spiritual leadership for the entire pioneer labor movement of the country. His philosophy is often referred to as "the religion of labor;" he preached as he practiced in his own life the creative therapy which a return to nature and physical work can bring to an over-intellectualized people. In the museum is a library containing Gordon's work and several thousand other books on agricultural themes. A different type of proud possession displayed by Degania is a *Renault tank* at its main entrance, one of a Syrian column stopped by Molotov cocktails as Degania's farmers threw back the attack of an army during the 1948 war.

Ein Gev. Eight miles past Degania, on the road which leads around the lake to the eastern shore and to the foot of the Mountains of Golan, is the village of Ein Gev, founded in 1937. Besides its success in agriculture, with banana plantations, and as a fishing village, Ein Gev has developed an annual Music Festival which brings tens of thousands of performers and audience each Passover to its huge concert hall. Ein Gev is a partner in the motor boat ferry cooperative which carries passengers to and fro across the lake. If you wish, you can take a boat from here back to Tiberias.

Around the Sea of Galilee, most of them along the lakeside near Tiberias, are many historical and religious sites revered by Judaism and Christianity. Of these the most important are Tabgha, Capernaum, the Mount of the Beatitudes, and Korazim.

Tabgha, 8 miles north of Tiberias, is the location of the ruins of the 4th–century *Church of the Multiplication of Loaves and Fishes.* Excavated in the nineteen thirties, the church is of interest mainly for its remarkable mosaic floor unearthed at that time. Tabgha is the traditional site of the miracle of the loaves and fishes, where Jesus fed the multitudes. The floor, 1,600 years old, has retained a brilliance that is remarkable. The colors are bright —and the workmanship superb. Near the altar built over the stone on which Jesus placed the fish and bread is a basket filled with loaves, and on either side a fish. Other parts of the mosaic floor show birds and plants of the region, fortress towers, and a round tower such as those used at the time to measure the rise and fall in the depth of the lake.

Capernaum (Kfar Nahum), barely 3 miles along the lake from Tabgha, is another spot revered by Christians. It was in and around Capernaum, a busy fishing port at the time, that Jesus spent most of the years after he fled from Nazareth. Several of the miracles of Jesus were performed here, and it was the home of a number of his disciples. The remains of a most handsome synagogue dating from the 3rd century A.D. have been excavated here.

On completing your tour of the sites around Tiberias, the best route to take in returning to Haifa is to continue along the road to Upper Galilee as far as Rosh Pina (from Tabgha to Rosh Pina is 8 miles), and then turn left to Safed (a further 6¼ miles). The drive through Meron and the Vale of Olives back to Haifa is another 46. If you decide to tour the whole of Upper Galilee, Safed is a good starting point.

SAFED AND
UPPER GALILEE

Rosh Pina is about 16 miles north of Tiberias. There is little distinctive for the visitor in this town, except from here begins the climb into the rare charm of the Galilean mountains. To its inhabitants, Rosh Pina is important because they are justly conscious of the town's pioneer role, even among the country's pioneers. It was the first Jewish settlement in Galilee and its oldest settlers will tell you that their parents started to clear the rock from a deserted piece of land in 1882. The climb up the mountains to Safed, a 6½ mile drive, rises to the highest plateau in Israel—some 2,800 feet above sea level. There are few spots anywhere in the country which match the view from this hilltop town sitting like a jeweled crown between mountain and sky. Nearing it, and looking down from the windows of car or bus, you will feel the urge to stop driving and exhaust the supply of film you have brought along.

Far below the crest, in the southeast, lies the Sea of Galilee, cradled on a clear day like a blue sapphire, guarded by the purple of the surrounding hills. To the northeast, is the shrunken Huleh Lake, a chip of the sapphire, and winding between them is the thinnest blue thread of the Jordan.

The small lake of Huleh is dominated in the background by the majestic white brow of Mount Hermon, snow-capped almost the entire year. Outside the country's northern border, the melting snows of the mountain pour down from its brow on to the Huleh Valley, feeding the Jordan River—the "Tears of Hermon."

To breathe the air of **Safed** is to appreciate why it is more than a summer resort or even a renowned health center. Perhaps its closeness to the sky made it so sacred in history. Everything below from here looks strictly mortal. Nor is it a wonder that Safed in modern times has added art, man's spirit in color, to its traditional mysticism. There is somehow a natural communion between the charm of its old cobbled streets and ancient synagogues and the beautifully wrought gardens and canvases of the painters.

Safed is one of Israel's ancient holy cities. Though it is not mentioned in early literature, the Roman Flavius Josephus reported that during the Jewish War against Rome he visited a place called Sepph. The Crusaders fortified the heights above the city in the 12th century A.D. It wasn't until the 16th century, however—practically yesterday by Israel standards—that Safed approached real historical prominence. At the end of the 15th and the beginning of the 16th centuries, due greatly to the pressures of the Spanish Inquisition, Safed became the refuge and the principal center of the Cabalists, an intellectual Jewish sect (which attracted a good number of Christians as well) which had worked out an intricate interpretation of the Bible, attaching mystic meaning to its every phrase, word, syllable, and letter—especially the four Hebrew letters in the word for God.

The two seminal books of the Cabalists were the *Sefer Yezirah* and the *Zohar,* the latter supposed to have been written by Rabbi Shimon Bar Yohai, whose tomb is at Safed, in the 2nd century A.D. The chief prophet of the Cabalists was Rabbi Izhak Lurie (Isaac Louria) who was known as "the Lion." Two of the several *Cabalistic synagogues* in Safed are identified with him: one of the Ashkenazim, and the other of the Sephardim. These and other places of worship stemming from the sect can be found by following a street that runs off to the left of the main street of the city, down the side of a sloping hill. It is best to go with a guide as you can easily miss several of them unless you know just where to look. The exterior architecture of all these synagogues is simple, but the design and interior work is brilliant and intricate. As you descend the hill you pass six synagogues of the Cabalists, ending with the Sephardic one associated with the Lion, at the foot of the hill opposite the town's ancient *cemetery*.

Safed, home of the ancient Cabalists

In the upper parts of the city there are many other sights of interest including the Citadel at the entrance to Safed. The *Citadel,* which was a point of resistance during the revolt against Rome in the 1st century A.D., was also the site of a Crusader stronghold. In 1948 it was stormed by Jewish fighters who routed a vastly superior force of Arabs. On the way to or from the Citadel, stop at the *Glicenstein Museum of Art* which contains the work of many of the local artists including Moshe Castel, Emmanuel Romano, and Aryeh Alweil.

Safed boasted the first printing press in Asia Minor (1578), which was used to make the first printed Hebrew book. It was the center of learning for all of Galilee for hundreds of years. For the modern visitor, however, its inherent charms mean more than ancient history. Today it is the place to which Israelis of the area flock to avoid the summer heat and enjoy the beauties of nature.

Before leaving Safed for Meron, there are a number of nearby villages worth visiting. There is, for example, the Moslem-Circassian hamlet of *Reihaniya,* whose inhabitants trace their origin to the shores of the Black Sea and whose children inherit from all preceding generations the dashing Circassian dances which their parents teach them as soon as they can walk. Near it is the village of *Alma* where people from the Italian village of San Nicandro settled when they embraced Judaism, following a visionary dream of one of their elders. In converting to Judaism, they left southern Italy to return "as the children of Israel to the Holy Land."

Just over 6 miles west of Safed is *Mount Meron,* and an orthodox village of that name founded in 1949. The *Shrine of Meron* is reached by a road branching off the highway to the right. It contains the cenotaphs of Rabbi Shimon Bar Yohai, the great Talmudic philosopher and patriot, and that of his son

Eleazar. The Lag B'Omer festival, which takes place each year 26 days after Passover, is celebrated here by hundreds of pilgrims each year.

The main highway circles Mount Meron on its way to *Rama,* 7½ miles away, and the road drops from the mountains almost 2,000 feet. You get glimpses on this road of round-topped Mount Tabor to the south and to the west a view of the Carmel. This is olive country *par excellence* with some of the finest trees in the country. To date, only the artist Reuben Rubin, among Israel's most talented painters, has been able to catch the soft silvery translucence of olive leaves which grow across this valley.

From Rama you follow the road down from the hills to Akko, about 18 miles, and then back to Haifa—another 15.

UPPER GALILEE

The 25 miles between Rosh Pina and Metulla skirts valley and mountain. Scenically, Upper Galilee is a rare and beautiful combination. West of the main road are the heights with the guardian settlements, *Manara* and *Yiftah,* perched above. At night their lights fuse with the twinkle of stars. East of the road, stretching to the Mountains of Bashan in Syria, is the *Huleh Valley and Lake*. The northernmost tip of Upper Galilee, from Kfar Giladi to Metulla, ends amid rolling hills and lovely woods. Striking in this entire area is the Jordan, beginning with its cold translucent spring source at Dan and winding its way south to the Lake. Ringing the valley through which it flows is the arched shield of villages, mounted on strategic sites.

On the way to Huleh, if interest in archaeology awakened around Tiberias still holds, there awaits **Hazor,** five miles north of Rosh Pina. It was identified as a Biblical site in 1928 by an expedition of the English University of Liverpool. Twenty-seven years later the dig began when a team of the Hebrew University opened the mound. The digging confirmed the Biblical evidence that the city was taken by Joshua from its Canaanite rulers. It was apparently a rich city for the Bible alludes to "much spoil" taken by the Israelites before they razed the city. Hazor is also mentioned as one of Solomon's chariot cities and the northern outpost that held together all of Galilee. The diggings have brought to light remnants from civilization back to the 14th century B.C., and ruins of what appears to have been Joshua's camp. **Huleh,** on a road to the east some 4 or 5 miles north of Hazor, is not much of its former self as a lake, and owes what it still has to the enthusiasm of the country's nature lovers, some whose affection leads them to hunt the wild boar and other game. In the early fifties almost the entire valley was a lake or swampland. Present fertile fields then lay under swamp and an abundance of papyrus weed. Only when the Jewish National Fund, described as "the major land reclamation agency of the country," blasted away the rocks impeding the Jordan's flow did the river amble tamely southward through canals. The marshes disappeared, and the lake receded, leaving thousands of beautiful new acres of additional real estate for the farmer. The spots of water, seen from the heights to the east were not overlooked, but are the artificial carp-breeding ponds of the villages. The Huleh drainage work was completed in 1957. On the eastern shore close to the Syrian border, is the village of *Ashmura,* which the Arabs call Dardara in their communiques after attack.

Returning to the Sdeh Eliezer crossroad, the highway continues north along the foot of the Galilean mountains to Kiryat Shmona and Metulla. Before Kiryat Shmona is a branch road leftwards which climbs up to the police fortress of *Nebi Yusha,* Arabic for the Prophet Joshua, and now called *Metsudat Koah.* The Hagana found it a tough nut to crack in the 1948 fighting. When you approach it you understand why. This is *the* magnificent and photogenic stand to view the valley below.

The fortress stands at a crossroads where a westward route branches off to *Kedesh Naftali* and the American-founded kibbutz of *Sasa,* and another heads south, passing the village of *Ramot Naftali* on its way to Safed. A third road, which shoots off northwards, mounts to *Yiftah, Ramin* (Manara), and another sky-high village—*Misgav Am.*

Taking this last fork, **Yiftah** is a little over a mile, and many drive up to the village to see its magnificent view. The kibbutz took its name from the brigade in which members fought against Lebanese and Syrians in 1948. Here, at the village, you literally rub shoulders with Lebanon.

The Tel Hai monument

At Margaliot the road encircles the ruins of a Crusader fortress called *Castrum Novum*—New Castle (without-the-coal). A right fork descends a steep slope to the Tel Hai monument and Kfar Giladi.

The **Tel Hai** monument, flanked by a youth hostel and Hagana museum commemorates a valiant stand in 1920 against a mass Arab attack. On a nearby hill are the graves of those who were killed. The memorial itself is a huge stone lion of Judah squatting on its haunches and was created by the Israeli sculptor Aaron Melnikov. Every year youth make a pilgrimage to pay tribute to the fighters who have become a modern symbol of resistance. Among the heroes buried here is Joseph Trumpeldor, commander of Tel Hai's defenders, and a national legend.

From Tel Hai it's a short distance back to the main road, and soon it forks left into Kfar Giladi (right to Metulla, the northernmost point of Israel). **Kfar Giladi,** named after one of the heroes of Tel Hai buried near the monument, is among the beauty spots of the country. Little wonder that its guest house is a popular summer resort, high in the hills, enveloped by lush greenery. In latter years, particularly for kibbutz villagers from all over the country, the dining hall of Kfar Giladi has been a permanent source of interest. Built to seat about 600 people in one shift, a controversy has preoccupied kibbutz planners and laymen as to whether a dining room should ever be so large. The kitchen at its rear has the facilities of a highly mechanized restaurant, surrounded by underground refrigeration rooms and a maze of mechanical cooking utensils and washing machines. The lawns around the huge dining hall are a beautiful place to laze, with the added enjoyment of the flower gardens. From here to Metulla and the border with Lebanon is but 2 miles. One of the proud roles played by Kfar Giladi is that since the early twenties Jews escaping from various forms of persecution, in choosing a northern entrance into Israel, have found the village their first welcome place of refuge and home. *Metulla* itself is a small border town of little interest. Founded in 1896, it sits on the edge of a valley known in the Bible as Iyon. Near it is the deep gorge of the river of that name where there is a waterfall almost enclosed by cliffs, because of its shape called *Tanur*—oven.

On the return southward along the main highway there is much to see on the left or east side of the road before coming again to the Huleh Lake. First is *Kiryat Shmona* (the town of eight) named by a new generation in honor of the defenders of nearby Tel Hai. Just a few years ago Kiryat Shmona was a ramshackle beehive of tin huts and improvised market stalls that made up a temporary immigrant intake camp. Yemenites and other newcomers built the houses and streets which now give it its new and permanent

One of the streams flowing into the Jordan River

look as a town. Most of its inhabitants farm in the valley, and they now run into thousands.

At Kiryat Shmona begins a side road to *Dafna* and *Dan* in the northern Huleh Valley. The latter is the major source of the Jordan. The Fountain of Dan is believed to have given the Jordan its name as a contraction of the two words *Yored-Dan* (descends from Dan). On a hot summer day this is the coolest part of Israel surrounded by the thick foliage of sturdy trees. It is a delightful picnic spot. The legends connected with Dan are endless and are in every guide book. In the Bible the national census was always referred to as being taken "from Dan to Beersheba."

Dan was captured by the tribe which moved up from the south: "Therefore the children of Dan went up to fight against Leshem, and took it, and smote it with the edge of the sword, and possessed it, and dwelt therein, and called Leshem, Dan, after the name of Dan their father." It was subsequently destroyed by an invasion described in the words of Jeremiah: "The snorting of his horses was heard from Dan: the whole land trembled at the sound of the neighing of his strong ones; for they are come, and have devoured the land, and all that is in it; the city, and those that dwell therein." The Arabs called the site Tel-el-Kadi, the Hill of the Judge, an echo, no doubt, of the role played by the Hebrew tribe: "Dan shall judge his people."

In the vicinity between Dan and Kiryat Shmona is the kibbutz village of *Ma'ayan Baruch,* settled in part by South African ex-servicemen and Americans, the cooperative of *Beit Hillel,* and *Hagoshrim* and *Dafna.* Between these two settlements, the waters of the Dan River and the rare old oak trees have been utilized to create a lovely National Park that will entice any traveler for a swim and picnic, or at least for a bite at the snack bar. From Dafna a road goes eastward over the River Banias, and beyond is the kibbutz of *Kfar Szold,* started in 1942, its name honoring Henrietta Szold, founder of the American Women's Zionist Organization, Hadassah. Near the Syrian border, 2 miles on, is another kibbutz, *Shamir,* so called after a tough unbreakable stone and the prophecy by Ezekiel: "Behold, I have made thy face strong against their faces . . . As an adamant (Shamir) harder than flint have I made thy forehead: fear them not, neither be dismayed at their looks . . ."

On the return journey to Rosh Pina and Safed there is a choice of two kibbutz villages built by settlers from Great Britain, both most interesting to visit. Traveling from north to south, the first is *Kfar Blum,* a union of English, American and Latvian settlers, which started in the thirties as the first pioneer outpost of British Zionists. The second, mostly consisting of members of the next generation of the movement, founded in England by the settlers of Kfar Blum, is *Kfar Hanasi.* The latter village was started in 1948 amidst a battle against Syrian invaders, as a defense point on a nearby height. Though Kfar Hanasi has done magnificently since then with its agriculture and large foundry, the seriousness of the fight for existence has not affected the reputation of its group as one of the most tolerant and humorous in the country. During festival time, its specialty is putting on satirical sketches. Unlike most kibbutz villages in Israel, its tolerance is expressed by the highly divergent political views of the inhabitants as politics, in the English tradition, "should not be taken over seriously." Rumor has it that most important here are the fish and chips and latest test-match scores—there is definitely no "pub." Besides the English, there is a sprinkling of Australians and New Zealanders from "Down Under."

The Hazor ruins—and beyond, the orchards of an upper Galilee kibbutz

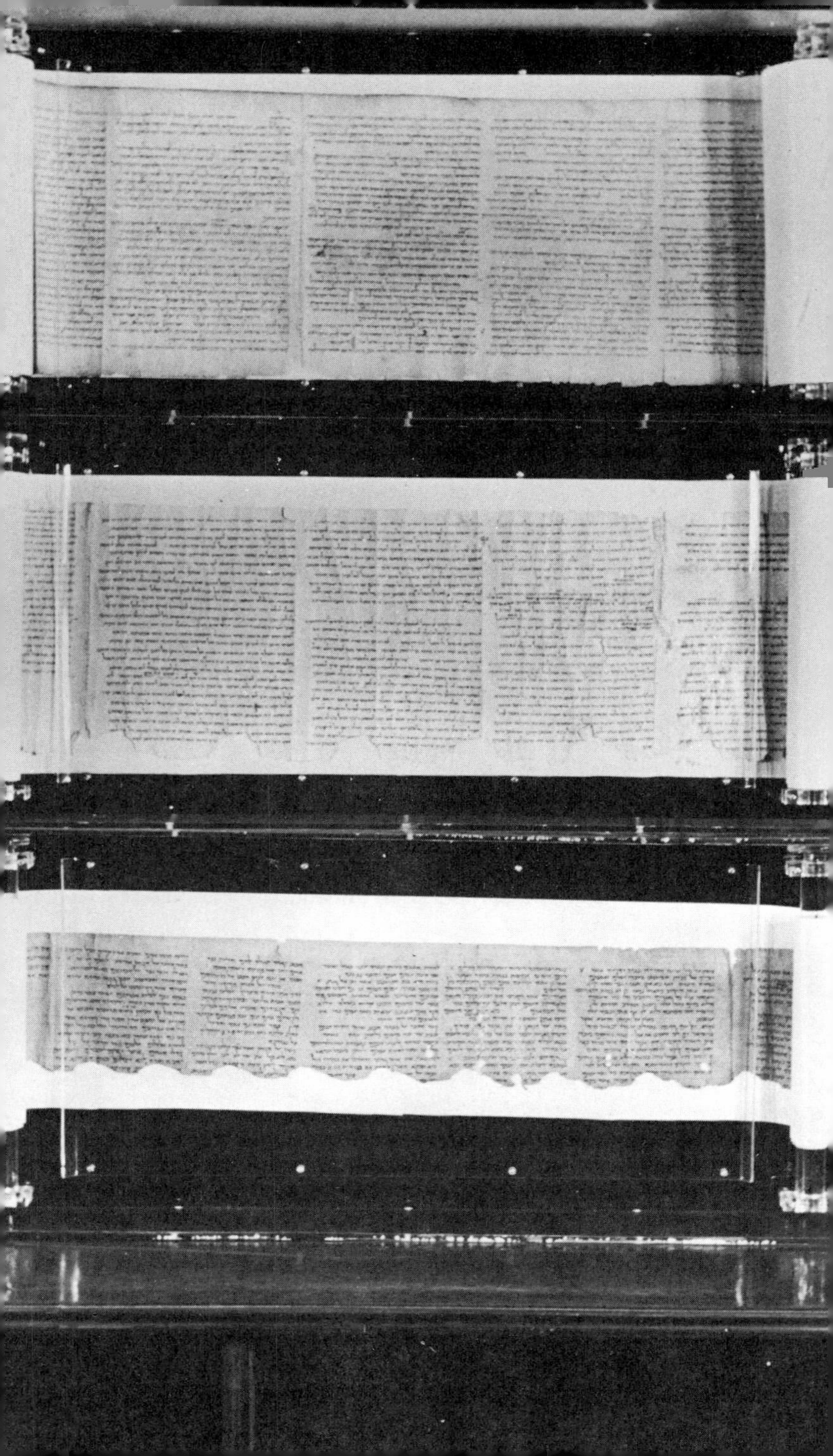

CHAPTER 7

Let no one tell you that Hebrew is an easy language to learn unless, of course, it happened to be your mother tongue. To start with, it is not a Latin script, reads from right to left and has a complicated though logical syntax. But though it is unlikely that you will attempt to learn the language as a preface to a short visit, common words and phrases can be absorbed. It will not only give you satisfaction but your reward will be in the pleasure of the Israelis. They are immensely pleased when visitors try to speak to them in their own tongue.

Pronunciation. The words in the following lists are spelled in English as they sound in the Hebrew. The accented syllable is in capitals. This is not always an exact transliteration but the simplest. Where you see 'h' or 'H' with a line under it, '<u>h</u>' or '<u>H</u>', it is pronounced like the 'ch' in Bach.

General

Peace (general greeting or farewell)	*sha-LOM*
Good Sabbath	*Sha-BAT sha-LOM*
Please	*b'vah-kah-SHAH*
Yes, no, perhaps	*ken; loh; oo-LIE*
Thank you (very much)	*toh-DAH (ra-BAH)*
You're welcome	*ahl loh da-VAR*
Good morning	*BO-ker tov*
Good night	*LIE-la tov*
What time is it?	*ma ha-sha-AH*
Pardon me	*slee-<u>H</u>AH*
How are you?	*ma <u>sh</u>lom-<u>H</u>A* (m)
	ma shlo-MAY<u>H</u> (f)

The Dead Sea Scrolls on display in Jerusalem

Fine, thank you	*tov to-DAH*
See you again	*le-hit-ra-OHT*
Where is . . .?	*eh-FOH*
What is this?	*ma zeh*
What do you wish?	*ma ah-TA ro-TSEH* (m)
	ma aht ro-TSAH (f)
I should like	*ah-NEE ro-TSEH* (m)
	ah-NEE ro-TSAH (f)
How much is it?	*KAH-mah zeh o-LEH*
I understand	*ah-NEE meh-VEEN* (m)
	ah-NEE me-vee-NAH (f)
I do not understand	*ah-NEE loh meh-VEEN* (m)
	ah-NEE loh me-vee-NAH (f)
I do not speak Hebrew	*ah-NEE loh m'da-BER iv-REET* (m)
	ah-NEE loh m'da-BEH-ret iv-REET (f)
Do you speak English?	*ha-IM ah-TA m'da-BER ang-LEET* (m)
	ha-IM aht m'da-BEH-ret ang-LEET (f)
What is this in Hebrew?	*ma zeh b'iv-REET*
Say it slowly please	*na le-da-BER le-ATT*
Write it down please	*na lih-TOV zoht*
What's to be done?	*ma la-ah-SOHT*
That is all	*zeh ha-KOL*
Wait a moment please	*REH-ga b'vah-kah-SHAH*
Is it open?	*ha-IM zeh pa-TOO-ah*
I cannot come	*ah-NEE loh ya-HOL la-VOH* (m)
	ah-NEE loh ye-hoh-LA la-VOH (f)
I am in a hurry	*ah-NEE mi-ma-HAYR* (m)
	ah-NEE mi-ma-HEH-ret (f)
I am cold	*KAHR lee*
I am hot	*HAHM lee*
Your health! (when drinking)	*le-HA-yim*
Good health!	*la-bree-OOT*
Congratulations!	*ma-ZAL tov*
What is your name?	*ayh koh-REEM le-HA* (m)
	ayh koh-REEM lah (f)
My name is . . .	*koh-REEM lee . . .*
I come from . . .	*ah-NEE bah mee . . .*
Where do you live?	*eh-FOH ah-TA gahr* (m)
	eh-FOH aht ga-RAH (f)
What do you do?	*bah-MEH ah-TA oh-VED* (m)
	bah-MEH aht oh-VEH-det (f)
I am a tourist	*ah-NEE ta-YAHR* (m)
	ah-NEE ta-YEHR-et (f)
Alright	*b'SAY-der*
To the right	*yeh-MEEN-ah*
To the left	*SMO-lah*
Straight ahead	*yah-SHAR*
Something	*Ma-sheh-hoo*
Nothing	*shoom da-VAR*
Enough	*mas-PEEK, dye*
More	*yoh-TEHR*

An open air market in Jerusalem

Less	*pa-HOHT*
Slowly	*le-ATT*
Quickly	*ma-HAYR*
At once	*mee-YAD*
Easy	*kahl*
Difficult	*kah-SHEH*
Family	*mish-pa-HAH*
Mommy	*EE-mah*
Daddy	*AH-bah*
Brother, sister	*ah, ah-HOHT*
Uncle, aunt	*dohd, doh-DA*
Boy	*YEH-led*
Girl	*yahl-DAH*
White	*la-VAHN* (m), *le-vah-NA* (f) *le-vah-NEEM* (pl)
Blue	*kah-HOL* (m), *ke-hoo-LA* (f) *ke-hoo-LEEM* (pl)
Summer	*KYE-itz*
Spring	*ah-VEEV*
Winter	*HOH-reff*
Autumn	*stav*

For Emergencies

I need a doctor (policeman)	*ah-NEE tsa-REEH roh-FEH (shoh-TEHR)* (m)
	ah-NEE tse-ree-HAH . . . (f)
Where is the drugstore?	*eh-FOH bet mir-KAH-hat*
Where is the restroom?	*eh-FOH ha-no-hi-YOOT*
Will you call the manager?	*na lik-RO et ha-me-nah-HAIL*
Will you call the American Consulate?	*na lik-RO et ha-con-SOO-lya ha-America-NEET*
Can I send a telegram?	*ha-oo-HAL lish-LOH-ah miv-RAK*
I have lost my wallet	*ee-BAH-d'tee et ha-ahr-NAK'she-LEE*

Hotels and Restaurants

Have you a room?	*yesh la-HEM HE-der pa-NOOI*
With a bathroom	*im ahm-BAT-yah*
What is the daily rate?	*ma ha-m'HEER le-YOHM*
What is the weekly rate?	*ma ha-m'HEER le-sha-VOO-ah*
Can I have a dress (suit) pressed?	*ha-IM ef-SHAR le-gah-HETS lee sim-LAH (ha-li-FAH)*
Please send the waiter	*na li-SHLO-ah et ha-mel-TSAR*
Please send the maid	*na li-SHLO-ah et ha-hahd-rah-NEET*
Where is the dining room?	*eh-FOH ha-DAR ha-OH-hel*
Where is the telephone?	*eh-FOH ha-tele-FON*
Where is the bar?	*eh-FOH ha-BAR*
What is the bill?	*ma ha-hesh-BON*
My key	*ha-maff-TAY-ah sheh-LEE*
Any messages for me?	*ha-IM yesh lee hoh-da-OT*
Where can I buy a newspaper?	*eh-FOH ef-SHAR lik-NOT ee-TOHN*
Who is there?	*mee shahm*
Come in	*he-ka-NESS* (m) *he-kan-SEE* (f)

Tower of David, Jerusalem

Come back later please	*na la-ha-ZOR yo-TEHR meh-oo-HAR*
Iced water	*MA-yeem kah-REEM*
Another towel please	*ohd ma-GEH-vet b'vah-kah-SHAH*
The menu please	*ha-taf-REET b'vah-kah-SHAH*
Writing paper	*ne-YAHR ke-tee-VAH*
Kosher	*kah-SHAIR*
Breakfast	*ah-roo-HAHT BO-ker*
Lunch	*ah-roo-HAHT tso-ho-RAH-yeem*
Dinner	*ah-roo-HAHT EH-rev*
Can we eat?	*ha-noo-HAHL leh-eh-HOL*
Where is there a good restaurant?	*eh-FOH yesh mees-ah-DA toh-VAH*
The soup is cold	*ha-ma-RAHK kar*
Please bring me hot tea	*na le-ha-VEE lee tay hahm*
Please bring me iced coffee	*na le-ha-VEE lee kah-FAY ka-FOO*
The food was good	*ha-OH-hel ha-YAH tov*

Tea	*tay*
Coffee	*kah-FAY*
Sugar	*soo-KAR*
Milk	*ha-LAHV*
Bread	*LEH-hem*
Butter	*hem-AH*
Salt	*MEH-lah*
Pepper	*pil-PEL*
Soup	*ma-RAHK*
Fruit soup	*meh-RAHK peh-ROHT*
Fish	*dahg*
Meat	*bah-SAHR*
Vegetables	*yeh-ra-KOHT*
Fresh salad	*sah-LAHD tah-REE*
Dessert (last course)	*ma-NA ah-ha-roh-NA*
Stewed fruit	*kom-POHT*
Fresh fruit	*peh-ROHT tree-YEEM*
Knife	*sah-KEEN*
Fork	*maz-LEG*
Spoon	*kahf*
Plate	*tsa-LA-hat*
Cup	*SEH-fel*
Glass	*koss*
Napkin	*ma-PEET*

On the Road

Go	*sah*
Stop	*ah-TSOHR*
Go slowly	*sah le-ATT*
Road under repair	*ha-de-REH b'tee-KOON*
Dangerous curve	*see-BOOV meh-soo-KAHN*
Is this the road to . . . ?	*ha-IM zoht ha-DEH—reh le . . .*
To the north	*tsa-FOH-na*
To the south	*da-ROH-ma*

Friends and relatives give a new settler joyous greetings

From the west	*mee-meez-RAH*
From the east	*mee-ma-ah-RAV*
Keep straight ahead	*sah ya-SHAHR*
Turn to left (right)	*pnay SMO-lah (y'MEE-nah)*
How many kilometers to . . .	*kah-ma kilo-MET-reem ahd . . .*
Police station	*ta-ha-NATT ha-meesh-ta-RAH*

Taxi, Bus and Train

The airport	*sdeh ha-te-oo-FAH*
The port	*ha-na-MAHL*
The railway station	*ta-ha-NATT ha-rahKEH-vet*
Train	*rah-KEH-vet*
Taxi	*mo-NEET*
The ticket office	*ha-koo-PAH*
Ticket	*car-TEESS*
Porter	*sah-BAL*
How much is a ticket to . . .?	*KAH-mah o-LEH car-teess le . . .*
One-way ticket only	*rak car-TEESS ha-LOH*
Round-trip ticket	*car-TEESS ha-LOH va-ha-ZOR*
Have you a timetable?	*ha-IM yesh le-HA LOO-ah zmah-NEEM*
Bus	*auto-BOOSS*
Driver	*neh-HAG*
Which bus goes to . . . ?	*EH-zeh auto-BOOSS noh-SAY-ah le . . .*
Do you go to . . . ?	*ha-IM ah-TA ma-GEE-ah le . . .*
How much does the trip cost?	*KAH-ma o-LAH ha-ne-see-AH*
Please tell me when to get off	*na le-ha–GEED lee eh-FOH la-REH–det*
Please call a taxi	*na le-haz-MEEN mo-NEET*
How far is it?	*ma ha-mer–HAK*
How long will it take?	*KAH-ma zmahn zeh yee-KAH*
Wait for me	*ha-KEH lee*
Stop here please	*ah-TSOR kahn be-va-ka-SHAH*
I have no change	*ain lee KESS-ef kah-TAHN*

Entertainment

Cinema	*kol-NO-ah*
Theater	*tay-ah-TROHN*

Nightclub	*ma-oh-DON LIE-la*
Ballet	*bah-LET*
Opera	*OH-peh-rah*
Concert	*kon-TSERT*
Art museum	*mu-zay-ON le-oh-ma-NOOT*
Folk dances	*ree-koo-DAY ahm*
I want tickets for . . .	*ah-NEE roh-TSEH kar-tee-SEEM le . . .*
When does the performance start?	*ma-TIE mat-hee-LA ha-ha-tsa-GAH*
When does it end?	*ma-TIE zeh nig-MAHR*
Where can we dance?	*eh-FOH ef-SHAR leer-KOHD*

Shopping—Post Office, Drugstore, Hairdresser

Where is the post office?	*eh-FOH ha-DOH-ar*
Please send by airmail	*na lish-LOH-ah b'DOH-ar ah-VEER*
Registered	*rah-SHOOM*
Airletter	*ee-GEH-ret ah-VEER*
Postcard	*gloo-YAH (s) gloo-YOHT (pl)*
Stamp	*bool (s) boo-LEEM (pl)*
Envelope	*ma-ah-ta-FAH*
Cable (telegram) form	*TOH-fess miv-RAHK*
Where can I buy . . .?	*eh-FOH oo-HAL lik-NOHT . . .*
Drugstore	*bet mir-KAH-hat*
Barber, hairdresser	*sah-PAR; mas-peh-RAH*
Shave	*gee-LOO-ah*
Haircut	*tees-POH-ret*
Appointment	*p'gee-SHAH*
Shampoo	*ha-fee-FAH*
Manicure	*ma-nee-KOOR*
Dentist	*roh-FEH shee-NAH-yeem*
Toothpaste	*meesh-HAHT shee-NAH-yeem*
Toothbrush	*meev-REH-shet shee-NAH-yeem*
Blades	*sah-kee-NAY gee-LOO-ah*
Shaving cream	*meesh-HAHT gee-LOO-ah*
Soap	*sah-BOHN*

Time

What time is it?	*ma ha-sha-AH*
It is one o'clock	*ha-sha-AH ah-HAHT*
It is two-thirty	*ha-sha-AH SHTA-yim va-HEH-tsee*
It is a quarter past three	*ha-sha-AH sha-LOSH va-REH-vah*
It is a quarter to four	*ha-sha-AH REH-va le-ar-BAH*
At noon	*ba-tso-ho-RAH-yim*
At midnight	*ba-ha-TSOT*
Today	*ha-YOHM*
Yesterday	*et-MOHL*
Tomorrow	*ma-HAR*
Last night	*EH-mesh*
Tonight	*ha-EHR-ev*
Next week	*ha-sha-VOO-ah ha-BAH*
Last week	*ha-sha-VOO-ah sheh-ah-VAR*

Next month	*ha-HO-desh ha-BAH*
A year ago	*leef-NAY sha-NAH*
Last month	*ha-HO-desh sheh-ah-VAR*
Next year	*le-sha-NAH ha-bah-AH*
Last year	*ha-sha-NAH sheh-ahv-RAH*
I have no time	*ain lee zman*
What is the date?	*ma ha-ta-a-REEH*

Days of the Week

Day (s)	*yohm, yah-MIM*
Week (s)	*sha-VOO-ah, sha-voo-OHT*
Month (s)	*HO-desh, ho-da-SHEEM*
Sunday	*yohm ree-SHOHN*
Monday	*yohm shay-NEE*
Tuesday	*yohm shlee-SHEE*
Wednesday	*yohm re-vee-EE*
Thursday	*yohm ha-mee-SHEE*
Friday	*yohm shee-SHEE*
Saturday	*yohm sha-BATT*

The Rockefeller Museum in Jerusalem

A view of Old Jerusalem

Months

January	*YAH-noo-ahr*
February	*FEB-roo-ahr*
March	*mairss*
April	*ah-PREEL*
May	*my*
June	*YOO-nee*
July	*YOO-lee*
August	*OH-goost*
September	*sep-TEM-ber*
October	*oc-TOH-ber*
November	*noh-VEM-ber*
December	*deh-TSEM-ber*

NUMBERS

	MASCULINE	FEMININE
1	*eh-HAHD*	*ah-HAHT*
2	*SHNAH-yim*	*SHTAH-yim*
3	*shlo-SHAH*	*sha-LOSH*
4	*ahr-bah-AH*	*ahr-BAH*
5	*ha-mee-SHAH*	*ha-MESH*
6	*shee-SHAH*	*shesh*
7	*shee-VAH*	*SHEH-vah*
8	*shmoh-NAH*	*shmoh-NEH*
9	*teesh-AH*	*TAY-shah*
10	*ah-sah-RAH*	*ESS-air*
11	*ah-HAD-ah-SAHR*	*ah-HAHT—ess-RAY*
12	*SHNAYM-ah-SAHR*	*SHTAYM-ess-RAY*
13	*shlo-SHAH-ah-SAHR*	*SHLOSH-ess-RAY*
14	*ahr-bah-AH-ah-SAHR*	*ahr-BAH-ess-RAY*
15	*hah-mee-SHAH-ah-SAHR*	*ha-MESH-ess-RAY*

16	*shee-SHAH-ah-SAHR*	*SHESH-ess-RAY*
17	*sheev-AH-ah-SAHR*	*SHVAH-ess-RAY*
18	*shmo-NAH-ah-SAHR*	*shmo-NEH-ess-RAY*
19	*teesh-AH-ah-SAHR*	*tshah-ess-RAY*
20	*ess-REEM*	*ess-REEM*
21	*ess-REEM v'eh-HAHD*	*ess-REEM v'ah-HAHT*
30	*shlo-SHEEM* (m & f)	
40	*ahr-bah-EEM* "	
50	*hah-mee-SHEEM* "	
60	*shee-SHEEM* "	
70	*sheev-EEM* "	
80	*shmo-NEEM* "	
90	*teesh-EEM* "	
100	*may-AH* "	
101	*may-AH-veh-eh-HAHD* (m)	
	may-AH-veh-ah-HAHT (f)	
200	*ma-TIE-yeem* (m & f)	
300	*shlosh may-OHT* "	
1000	*EH-leff* "	
2000	*al-PIE-yeem* "	

	MASCULINE	FEMININE
First	*ree-SHOHN*	*ree-shoh-NAH*
Second	*shay-NEE*	*shnee-YAH*
Third	*shlee-SHEE*	*shlee-SHEET*
Fourth	*re-vee-EE*	*re-vee-EET*
Fifth	*ha-mee-SHEE*	*ha-mee-SHEET*
Sixth	*shee-SHEE*	*shee-SHEET*
Seventh	*shvee-EE*	*shvee-EET*
Eighth	*shmee-NEE*	*shmee-NEET*
Ninth	*tshee-EE*	*tshee-EET*
Tenth	*ah-see-REE*	*ah-see-REET*

VOCABULARY

Useful Nouns

Synagogue	*bet KNE-set*
Mosque	*miss-GAD*
Church	*knay-see-YAH*
Ashtray	*ma-ah-fay-RAH*

Israeli stamps commemorating Rosh Hashana 5718

Aspirin	*ah-spee-REEN*
Bobby-pins	*see-KOHT rosh*
Camera	*mahts-lay-MA*
Candies (sweets)	*soo-kah-ree-OHT*
Chair	*kee-SAY*
Chocolate	*shoh-ko-LAHD*
Class (in school)	*kee-TAH*
Cork	*pkak*
Friends	*ye-dee-DEEM*
Glasses (eye)	*meesh-ka-FAH-yim*
Ice cream	*glee-DA*
Letter	*meeh-TAHV*
Map	*ma-PA*
Matches	*gaff-roo-REEM*
Money	*KEH-seff*
Needle	*MA-hat*
Passport	*dar-KOHN*
Pin	*see-KAH*
School	*bet SAY-fer*
Scissors	*mees-pa-RAH-yim*
Shoelace	*sroh-NA-al*
Table	*shul-HAHN*
Thermometer	*mahd-HOHM*
Thimble	*ets-bah-OHN*
Thread	*hoot*
Toilet paper	*nee-YAHR twa-LET*
Washcloth	*mat-LEET*
Watch (wrist)	*sha-OHN*

Articles of Clothing

Coat	*me-EEL*
Sweater	*SVEH-dehr*
Jacket	*jah-KET*
Hat	*KOH-vah*
Shoes	*na-a-LA-yim*
Socks	*gar-BA-yim*
Nylons	*GAR-bay NY-lon*
Trousers	*mih-na-SA-yim*
Underwear	*le-va-NEEM*
Shirt	*hool-TSAH*
Panties	*tah-toh-NEEM*
Dress	*seem-LA*
Handbag	*ar-NAHK*
Belt	*ha-goh-RAH*
Tie	*ah-nee-VAH*

Parts of the Body

Face	*pa-NEEM*
Eyes	*ay-NA-yim*
Ears	*oz-NA-yim*
Mouth	*peh*

Head	*rosh*
Hair	*sah-ah-ROHT*
Neck	*tsa-VAHR*
Arms, hands	*ya-DA-yim*
Body	*goof*
Legs, feet	*rag-LA-yim*
Nails	*tsee-por-NA-yim*

Personal Pronouns

I, I am	*ah-NEE*
You, you are	*ah-TA* (m)
	aht (f)
He, he is	*hoo*
She, she is	*hee*
We, we are	*ah-NAH-noo*
You, you are	*ah-TEM* (m pl.)
	ah-TEN (f pl.)
They, they are	*haym* (m pl.)
	hayn (f pl.)

Prepositions, Adverbs

This	*ha-ZEH* (m) *ha-ZOHT* (f)
That	*ha-HOO* (m) *ha-HEE* (f)
These	*ha-AY-leh*
Those	*ha-HEM* (m) *ha-HEN* (f)
Who	*mee*
As, like	*k'MOH*
By, near	*le-YAHD*
With	*im*
From	*min*
Of	*shel*
Without	*b'lee*
To	*el*
In	*b' . . .*
What	*mah*
Again	*ohd PA-ahm*
Already	*k'vahr*
Also	*gahm*
Always	*ta-MEED*
Before, in front of	*leef-NAY*
Behind, after	*ah-hah-RAY*
But	*ah-VAL*
Here	*kahn*
How	*ayh*
Now	*ah-SHAHV*
Later	*yo-TEHR meh-oo-HAR*
Often	*le-ee-TEEM kroh-VOHT*
On	*ahl*
Only	*rak*
Since	*may-AHZ*
Soon	*beh-kah-ROHV*
Then	*ahz*

CHAPTER 8

Accommodations for visitors to Israel range from those offered by luxury hotels to those of modest but comfortable pensions and guest houses of the kibbutzim. Hotels are classified by the government according to a five star scale, which is maintained in the listing here. Five stars (*****) represents de luxe accommodations, four stars (****) first class. These two classes are of the highest international standards. The others, in declining order, meet the standards of international tourism but have fewer amenities. Two and one star hotels are generally family hotels and pensions. Most kibbutz guest houses are in the three to two star category.

Five and four star hotels are fully air-conditioned, with nearly all rooms having private baths. Three star hotels contain many rooms with private bath or shower, and some are air-conditioned. The two and one star hotels generally provide rooms with hot and cold water. Some have private showers; a few, private baths.

All Israeli hotels include breakfast with the price of the room, and many also offer half-board accommodations, breakfast and lunch or dinner. Remember that the rates in each category are subject to a good deal of variation from hotel to hotel. Customarily, a 10 per cent service charge is added to all hotel bills, thus obviating the need for tipping. For meals and drinks served in private rooms, a small "room service" charge is usual in most hotels.

A publication called "Israel Tourist Hotel Rates" is issued an-

The Dome of the Rock on the Temple Mount in Jerusalem

nually by the Israel Caterers' Association, and gives full particulars on all hotels recommended by the Israel Ministry of Tourism. It is obtainable free of charge from any Government Tourist Information Office or travel agency.

The table below will give you a reasonably accurate idea of the going rates. Prices are *per person,* based on the charge for bed and breakfast in a *double room* occupied by two people. The rates vary according to the season: peak, regular or winter. However, the peak season falls at different times of the year in different locations. For instance, in Tiberias and Eilat the peak rates are in effect during the winter. Rates are given in Israeli pounds. To get an approximate equivalent in dollars, divide by three and one half.

	Per Person **Peak/Regular**	*Bed and Breakfast* **Winter**
Five star	35–41	27–36
Four star	22–23	19–20
Three star	18–19	16–17
Two star	17	14
One star	8–10	7–8

The hotels listed are all recommended by the Ministry of Tourism. The symbol (K) after each indicates that the dietary laws are observed. Other symbols are as follows: (FA) stands for fully air-conditioned, (AR) stands for air-conditioned rooms, (S) indicates the presence of a swimming pool. The number of rooms in each hotel listed is also followed by the abbreviation (b.) or (sh.) denoting private bath or shower. Except where no board is indicated, all the hotels offer at least one combination, that is, room and full board, room and half board, room and breakfast, and most offer all three or at least two alternatives.

Restaurants listed are also approved by the Ministry of Tourism. The price of a three-course meal in a first-class restaurant will run from about $3.00 to $7.50. The medium-price range is about $1.50 to $3.00. Popularly priced places charge about $1.00 to $1.50. In the lists below (K) denotes kosher (dietary laws).

A listing of the kibbutzim having guest houses and of the Youth Hostels and the Christian Hospices, all with rates, follows the hotel-restaurant-shopping guide.

Among the citizens of Acre are fishermen who cast their nets in the Mediterranean. These walls withstood the siege guns of Napoleon.

Ashkelon-on-the-Sea (pop. 37,000)

HOTELS: ****Dagon, Afridar, 52 rooms (20 b., 32 sh.) (AR, S); ***Ashkelon, Afridar, 23 rooms (6 b., 17 sh.) (K); **Semadar, 24 rooms (4 b., 20 sh.); *Shimshon Gardens, 30 Hatamar St., 22 rooms (5 b., 17 sh.) (K).

SHOPPING: Bezalel arts and crafts, other souvenirs and gifts at Ashkelon Pavilion.

USEFUL ADDRESSES: Tourist Information Office, New Commercial Center; Bank Leumi Le-Israel, New Commercial Center.

Beersheba (pop. 72,000)

HOTELS: ****Desert Inn, 120 rooms (120 b.) (K, FA, S); ***Zohar, 47 rooms (42 b., 5 sh.) (K, AR); **Ein Gedi, 43 rooms (35 sh.) (AR); **Hanegey, 22 rooms (22 sh.) (K, FA); *Arava, 27 rooms (2 b., 25 sh.) (K, AR); *Aviv, 18 rooms (18 sh.) (AR); *Roll, 28 rooms (28 sh.) (AR).

NIGHT CLUBS: The Sheikh's Tent, at the Desert Inn Hotel. The setting is a genuine Bedouin tent, the food appropriately eastern and excellent. Evening entertainment is derived from both East and West.

MUSEUM: The Negev Museum, archaeological finds of the region, Bedouin folklore.

USEFUL ADDRESSES: Tourist Information Office, Beit Ha'am; Bank Leumi Le-Israel, Ha'atzmaut St.; Israel Discount Bank Ltd., 62 Histadrut St.

Caesarea Resort Area

HOTELS: ****The Caesarea (Operated by the Club Mediterannee) 110 rooms (110 b.) (K, FA, S). A primary attraction is the golf course. ****Semadar Villa (A1), 54 apartments (54 b.) (K, FA, S).

RESTAURANT: Stratton, at old Roman port, dinner and dancing under the stars.

Eilat (pop. 12,000); on the Red Sea

HOTELS: ****Eilat, 30 rooms (24 b., 11 sh.) (FA, K); ****Queen of Sheba, 89 rooms (65 b., 24 sh.) (K, FA, S); ****Neptune, 98 rooms (98 b.) (K, FA); ****Red Rock, 74 rooms (74 b.) (K, FA, S); ****Solomon, 48 rooms (48 b.) (K, FA); **Caravan, 72 rooms (72 sh.) (K, AR); **Oasis (motel), 24 rooms (24 sh.) (K, FA); **Ophir, 33 rooms (5 b., 28 sh.) (AR); **Red Sea, 41 rooms (2 b., 39 sh.) (K, FA); **Sahara, 26 rooms (26 sh.) (K, AR).

NIGHT CLUB: Red Rock Night Club, located, naturally, in the Red Rock Hotel.

SHOPPING: Eilat gems, jewelry, souvenirs, all photographic services at Photo Eilat.

MUSEUM: Red Sea Museum, flora and fauna, especially tropical fish, of the Red Sea.

USEFUL ADDRESSES: Government Tourist Information Office, Airport Bldg.; Bank Leumi Le-Israel, Business Center.

Ein Bokek (Dead Sea)

HOTEL: *Ein Bokek Guest House, 32 rooms (20 sh.) (K, AR).

Haifa (pop. 212,000)

Haifa Town

HOTELS: ****Zion, 5 Baerwald St., 94 rooms (89 b., 5 sh.) (FA, K); ***Appinger, 28-30 Carmel Ave., 26 rooms (9 b., 11 sh.); ***Carmelia Court, 35 Herzliya St., 51 rooms (15 b., 30 sh.) (K, AR); **Nesher, 53 Herzl St., 15 rooms (10 sh.); **Talpioth, 61 Herzl St., 24 rooms (2 b., 15 sh.) (AR); *Weiss, 2 Shmaryahu Levin St., 50 rooms (42 sh.) (K); *Windsor, 14–16 Carmel Ave., 27 rooms (2 b., 3 sh.) (K).

David's Tower, located near the Jaffa Gate, in Jerusalem

Haifa Mt. Carmel (alt. 960 ft.)

HOTELS: *****Dan Carmel, 222 rooms (222 b.) (K, FA, S); ****Shulamith, 69 rooms (50 b.) (K, AR); ***Dvir, 35 rooms (33 b., 2 sh.); ***Ben Yehuda, 154 Sea Rd., 63 rooms (31 b., 31 sh.) (S); **Hod MaCarmel, 17 Elhanan St., 23 rooms (9 b., 13 sh.) (K); **Korngold, 3 Smolenskin St., 13 rooms (10 b.) (AR); **Lev HaCarmel, 22 Heine Sq., 46 rooms (18 b., 25 sh.); **Shoshanat HaCarmel, 90 Shoshanat Ha-Carmel St., 35 rooms (7 b., 20 sh.); **Wohlman, 16 Sea Rd., 10 rooms (2 b., 4 sh.); *Lea, 14 Sderot Habroshim, 10 rooms (1 b., 4 sh.).

RESTAURANTS: Balfour Cellar (FA, K), 3 Balfour St., European food; Bilu Cellar, 2 Bank Street; Carmel, 125 Hanassi Ave.; Florida, 16 Nordau St.; Gan Armon, 16 Haneviim St.; Gan Rimon, 16 Sderot Habroshim, European food; Gil, 35 Moriah St.; Hadar, 6 Baerwald St., European; Korngold, 64 Ha'atzmaut and 10 Nordau St., Kosher cuisine; Pross, 17 Sderot HaCarmel, both Oriental and European style cooking; Ritz, 5 Haim St.; Prust Restaurant, Sderot HaCarmel, European cuisine; Ron, 139 Sderot Hanassi, European; San Remo, 23 Herzl St.; Cafe Snir, 27 Herzl St., famous for pastries, special ice creams, Espresso bar.

NIGHT CLUBS: The Zion Hotel supplies a band for dancing; the Ramat Hadar offers floor shows; the Gan Rimon, Pross and the Shoshanat HaCarmel Hotel have music and dancing. Also The Rondo, Dan Carmel Hotel and Rothschild's Cellar, gathering place for young people.

MUSEUMS: Museum of Ancient Art, City Hall, Bialik St., coins, pottery, bronze tools, mosaics, etc.; Museum of Japanese Art, 89 Shderot Hanasi; Museum of Modern Art, City Hall, permanent exhibition of local art, also has loan exhibitions; Beit Chagall, 32 U.N. Ave., offers one-man shows and collective exhibitions of modern Israel art; Maritime Museum, 2 Hanamal St., displays an exhibition on Israel's seafaring history and Jewish underground immigration (Aliya Bet); Biological Institute and Museum of Natural Sciences, Gan Ha'em, Central Carmel, features natural science exhibits and a small zoo; Ethnological Museum and Folklore Archives, 19 Arlosoroff St.; Artists' Village Ein Hod, on the outskirts of Haifa, houses a colony of painters, sculptors and craftsmen. Special exhibitions and programs are held regularly.

SHOPPING: Yemenite handwork, souvenirs and gifts: J. D. Bassan, 40 Herzl St.; Ben-Hillel, 18 Horeb Sq.; Bezalel Shop, 45 Herzl St.; Engelstein Ltd., 39 Herzl St.; K. Hetsroni, 16 Herzl St.; Pardo, 6 Palmer's Gate; Pinati, 29 Nordau St.; Wizo Shops, 9 Nordau St. Toys and sporting goods: Pinochio, 1 Balfour St.; A. Soloweitchik, 3 Balfour St. Perfumes: Harry Wachs, 19 Herzl St. Flowers: Ginsburg & Sons, 20 and 44 Herzl St.; Nitza, 4 Nordau St. Leather goods: Hirsch's Leather Shop, 35 Jaffa Rd.; M. Mais & Co., 27 Herzl St. Jewelry: A. Muenz, 1 Balfour St. Furs: Kuhnreich Bros., 48 Herzl St. Children's wear: Zabar, 2 Balfour St. Clothing: Boutique Siegl, Central Carmel; Dan Gabrieli Ltd., 18-20 Herzl St.; Donna, 21 Herzl St.; Freund, Central Carmel; Salma, 20 Herzl St. Books and music: H. Blumenthal, 1 Herzl St. Art and antiques: Goldman's Art Gallery,

92 Sd. Hanassi; Traclin Art Gallery, 4 Baerwald St.

USEFUL ADDRESSES: *Tourist Information Office,* 16 Herzl St. and Shed No. 12 and No. 14 in Haifa Port; *Main post office,* 82 H'atzmaut Rd.; *Telegraph office,* 3 N'tiv Yosef; *Bank Leumi Le-Israel,* 20 Jaffa Rd. (main office); *Israel Discount Bank Ltd.,* 47 Ha'atzmaut Rd. and 34 Herzl St.

Herzliya-on-the-Sea (pop. 36,000); near Tel Aviv.

HOTELS: *****Accadia Grand Hotel,* 194 rooms (191 b.) (FA, K, S); *****Sharon,* 150 rooms (91 b., 50 sh.) (FA, K, S); ***Hod,* 30 rooms (30 b.) (K, AR); ***Tadmor,* 60 rooms (39 b., 21 sh.) (K, AR); ***Validor,* 31 rooms (25 b., 2 sh.) (K, AR, S); **Cymberg,* 11 rooms (5 b., 2 sh.); *Varda,* 9 rooms (K).

The *Accadia* and the *Sharon* both have fine dining rooms serving excellent food.

NIGHT CLUBS: The *Accadia Hotel Bar* offers a band with a singer and dancing as does the *Topaz Bar* in the Tadmor Hotel.

USEFUL ADDRESSES: Israel Discount Bank Ltd., Chen Blvd.

Jerusalem (pop. 275,000); (alt. 2,600 ft.)

Eastern Jerusalem (Old City and suburbs)

HOTELS: *****Intercontinental,* Mount of Olives, 202 rooms (202 b.); *****Mount Scopus,* Sheikh Jarach, 52 rooms (52 b.); *****Saint George,* St. George St., 150 rooms (150 b.); ****Holyland,* Rashid St., 80 rooms (80 b.); ****Panorama,* at foot of Mount of Olives, 74 rooms (71 b., 3 sh.); ****National Palace,* AzZahra St., 103 rooms (80 b., 17 sh.) (AR); ****American Colony,* Nablus Rd., 70 rooms (55 b., 15 sh.); ***YMCA,* Nablus Rd.; ***Gloria,* Latin Patriachate St., 64 rooms (63 b.); ***Shepherd,* Mount of Olives Road, 52 rooms (52 b).

RESTAURANTS: *Hassan Effendi; Jerusalem Oriental; Golden Chicken.*

NIGHT CLUBS: *Le Cave; Le Cave des Rois.*

New Center

HOTELS: *****King David,* King David St., 270 rooms (270 b.) (K, FA, S); ****Eden,* Hillel St., 36 rooms (26 b., 10 sh.) (K, FA); ****Kings,* 60 King George Ave., 147 rooms (147 b.) (K, FA); ****President,* 3 Ahad Ha'am St., 91 rooms (64 b., 24 sh.) (K, S); ***YMCA,* 26 King David St., 71 rooms; **Grete Asher,* 14 rooms (12 b., 2 sh.) (K); **OrGil,* Hillel St., 58 rooms (9 b., 18 sh.) (K); **Palatin,* 3 Agrippas St., 23 rooms (14 sh.) (K); **Ron,* Jaffa St., 15 rooms (6 sh.) (K); *Vienna,* 2 Lunz St., 17 rooms (3 sh.).

Jerusalem Resort Area

HOTELS: *****Diplomat,* 386 rooms (386 b.) (K, FA, S); ****Holyland,* 60 rooms (56 b., 4 sh.) (K, FA, S); ****Judea Gardens,* 76 rooms (76 b.) (K, FA, S); ***Reich,* 54 rooms (51 b., 3 sh.) (K); ***Margoa,* 34 rooms (30 b., 4 sh.) (K); **Har Aviv,* 25 rooms (13 b., 9 sh.) (K); **Rama-Gidron House,* 20 rooms (6 b., 6 sh.); *Eden*, 6 rooms (2 b., 4 sh.) (K).

RESTAURANTS: *Dekel* (K), 44 Jaffa Rd., Oriental dishes; *Pfefferberg* (K), European cooking, famous for gefilte fish; *Fink's*, 13 King George Ave., European; *Dolphin*, Rashidiya St., seafood; *Goulash Inn*, Ein Karem, Hungarian cuisine; *Goldschmidt's* (K), 3 Dorot Rishonim St., European; *Gondola*, 14 King George Ave., good Italian food; *Hefner*, 4 Lunz St., European; *Hesse* (K), Ben Shatah St., European; *Mandarin*, 2 Shlomzion Hamalka St., Chinese and European food; *My Bar*, 12 Hillel St., European; *Palmachi*, 13 Shamai St., Oriental; *Rimon*, Dorot Rishonim St., Oriental (K); *Shemesh*, 21 Ben Yehuda St., Oriental; *Sinai*, 6 Ben Yehuda St., Oriental; *Yerushalayim* (K), Jaffa Rd., cnr. Straus, European.

NIGHT CLUBS: The *President Hotel Bar*, the *King David Hotel Bar*, and the *Mandarin* have small orchestras for dancing; *My Bar* and the *Gondola* have dancing to record music; other night spots are *Fink's Bar*, the *Bacchus*, and the *Saramello*.

MUSEUMS AND LIBRARIES: The *Israel Museum*, comprising the *Bezalel National Art Museum*, *Samuel Bronfman Museum of Archaeology;* the *Billy Rose Art Garden* (sculptures), and the *Shrine of the Book* (Dead Sea Scrolls); *Jewish National and University Library*, on the new Hebrew University campus; *Yeshurun Library*, King George Ave. (in Yeshurun Synagogue), Hebraica and Judaica and modern Hebrew books; *Schocken Library*, Balfour St., Talbieh, private collection including incunabulae, drawings and lithographs; *Knesset Library*, Knesset Bldg., official Israel document collection; *Y.M.-C.A. Library*, King David St.; *Palestine Archaeological* (Rockefeller Museum), opp. Herod's Gate, East Jerusalem; *Pontifical Biblical Library*, Paul Emile Botta St., Biblical and Oriental library and archaeological museum administered by Jesuits; *Jerusalem Biblical Zoo*.

SHOPPING: *Souvenirs and gifts:* Bachner, 11a Ben Yehuda St.; Baltinester Bros., 27 Jaffa Rd.; Charlotte, 4 Koresh St.; Doron, 27 Jaffa Rd.; Idit Arts & Crafts, 16 Ben Yehuda St.; Iran Bazaar, 3 Ben Yehuda St.; Moshe Gift Shop, King David Hotel Lobby; Saenger's Gift Shop, 11 Hapoalim St. Shlagman, 4 Dorot Rishonim St.; Souvenir Center, Egged Bldg., Zion Sq.; "Suzyn", 6 Shlomzion Hamalka St.; Teheran Bazaar, 4 Ben Yehuda St.; Wizo Shops, 34 Jaffa Rd. *Toys:* Snow White Toys (Shilgia), Zion Sq. *Clothing:* Beer & Sons, 45 Jaffa Rd.; Epstein & Felheim, 50 Jaffa Rd.; Heilig & Co., Shlomzion Hamalka St.; C. I. Levy Ltd., "The Pillars," Jaffa Rd.; B. Rosenblum Ltd., 3 Shlomzion Hamalka St.; Stock & Co., 3 Ben Yehuda St. *Furs:* Scharf's Furs Ltd., "The Pillars," Jaffa Rd.; Wolf's Furs, 1 King George Ave. *Shoes:* Comfort-Comfy, 22 Ben Yehuda St.; Freiman & Bein, "The Pillars," Jaffa Rd.; Gil 51 Jaffa Rd. *Leather goods:* Pinati, 8 Ben Yehuda St. *Jewelry:* Adi, 1 Straus St.; I. Baida, 10 King George Ave.; Gaber, 1 King George Ave.; R. Moussaieff & Sons Ltd., 2 Shlomzion Hamalka St.; Shorr, 19 King George Ave.; Switzeria, 11 King George Ave. *Flowers:* Dalia Flowers, 27 King George Ave. *Books and music:* Radiophone Record Shop, 6 Ben Yehuda St.; Saphir, 2 Ben Yehuda

A nun of the Franciscan convent on the Mount of Beatitudes looks out over the Sea of Galilee

St.; University Campus Bookshop, Hebrew University. *Photographic services:* Photo Eden, 3 Ben Yehuda St.; Photo Stern, 7 King George Ave. *Artwork and antiques:* Rina Art Gallery, 13 Shlomzion Hamalka St.; Safrai Art Gallery, 37 Jaffa Rd.; Joshua Simon, King David Hotel Annex.

USEFUL ADDRESSES: *Tourist Information Office,* 24 Rehov Hamelech George, and Jaffa Gate; *General Post Office and Philatelic Services,* 23 Jaffa Rd., *Bank Leumi Le-Israel,* 21 Jaffa Rd. (main office); *Israel Discount Bank Ltd.,* 11 Ben Yehuda St. *Beauty parlors,* Kramer's, 1 Ben Yehuda St.; Salon Broadway, 36 Ben Yehuda St., Salon Robert, King George Ave.

Kiryat Tivon (pop. 9,200); (Haifa telephone exchange)

HOTELS: **Nave,* 23 rooms (1 b., 18 sh.) (K, AR); **Paula Pick,* 22 rooms (2 b., 17 sh.); *Seidler,* 9 rooms (6 sh.); *Shalva,* 17 rooms (2 b., 9 sh.); *Sternberg,* 11 rooms (11 sh.) (K); *Vered,* 27 rooms (24 sh.) (K).

Lod Airport Area (Tel Aviv telephone exchange)

HOTELS: *****Avia,* 100 rooms (100 b), no board, restaurant and cafeteria. (FA, K, S); its *Jet Club* offers music and dancing, and its souvenir shop is duty free.

USEFUL ADDRESS: *Tourist Information Office* in Airport Bldg.

Nahariya-on-the-Sea (pop. 20,700)

HOTELS: *****Carlton,* 75 rooms (60 b., 15 sh.) (K, FA, S); ****Astar,* 26 rooms (26 b.) (FA); ****Frank,* 28 rooms (28 sh.) (K, AR); ***Rosenblatt,* 37 rooms (37 sh.) (K); ***Eden,* 46 rooms (44 sh.) (AR); ***Galei Yam,* 21 rooms (20 b., 1 sh.) (K); ***Lau-fer,* 46 rooms (46 sh.) (AR); ****Rosenshein,* 15 rooms (15 sh.) (AR); **Silberman,* 15 rooms (12 sh. (K).

RESTAURANTS AND NIGHT CLUBS: *Freddy's Inn,* meals, dancing, entertainment. The *Penguin* serves sturdy food of the Teutonic variety and offers a floor show with a band for dancing. The *Weidenbaum Pension* has dancing to record music.

SHOPPING: Bezalel gifts at *Matanot,* 30 Ga'aton Blvd.

USEFUL ADDRESSES: *Bank Leumi Le-Israel,* Ga'aton Blvd.; *Israel Discount Bank Ltd.,* Ga'aton Blvd.

Natanya-on-the-Sea (pop. 60,000)

HOTELS: *****Four Seasons,* 129 rooms (129 b.) (K, FA, S); ****Grand Yahalom,* 36 rooms (36 b.) (K, FA); ****Metropol Grand,* 36 rooms (30 b., 6 sh.) (K, FA); ***Galei Zans,* 82 rooms (82 b.) (K, AR); ***Gan Hammelech,* 47 rooms, (39 b., 8 sh.) (K, AR); ***Hadar,* 33 rooms (18 b., 15 sh.) (K, AR, S); ***Palace,* 71 rooms (44 b., 27 sh.) (K, FA); **Almog,* 22 rooms (22 sh.) (K); **Ast,* 25 rooms (5 b., 20 sh.) (K, AR); **Armon,* 31 rooms (31 sh.) (K, AR); **Ein Hayam,* 45 rooms (45 sh.) (K, AR); **Gal Yam,* 22 rooms (4 b., 18 sh.) (K); **Galei Hasharon,* 24 rooms (24 sh.) (K); **Gil,* 23 rooms (8 b., 15 sh.) (K); **Ginot Yam,* 36 rooms (36 sh.) (K); **Greenstein,* 37 rooms (14 b., 23 sh.) (K); **Hof,* 20 rooms (20

View of Tel Aviv seashore from tower of St. Peter's Church in Jaffa

sh.) (K, AR); **Margoa,* 33 rooms (8 b., 25 sh.) (K, AR); **Metropol,* 27 rooms (6 b., 21 sh.) (K, FA); **Savyon,* 39 rooms (15 b., 24 sh.) (K); **Talmor,* 25 rooms (6 b., 19 sh.) (K); **Win-kelberg,* 10 rooms (4 b., 6 sh.); *Daphna,* 16 rooms (16 sh.) (K); *Ofakim* (C1), 30 rooms (30 sh); *Shaket* (C1), 16 rooms (16 sh.) (K).

SHOPPING: *Gifts, including Bez-alel work:* "Hadar," 5 Herzl St. *Books:* A. Pompan, 9 Herzl St. *Clothing:* Mergler, 18 Herzl St.; Salon Edith, 15 Herzl St.

USEFUL ADDRESSES: *Bank Leumi Le-Israel,* 5 Herzl St.; *Israel Discount Bank Ltd.,* 26 Zion Sq. Israel's golf course is nearby at ancient *Caesarea.*

Nazareth (pop. 32,000); (alt. 1,200 ft.)

HOTEL: ***Grand New Hotel,* 54 rooms (24 b., 30 sh.) (AR); ***Nazareth,* 52 rooms (29 b., 23 sh.); *Hagalil,* 31 rooms (4 b.) (K).

RESTAURANTS: *Abu Nasser; As-toria, Israel; Riviera.*

USEFUL ADDRESSES: *Government Tourist Information Office,* Casanova St.; *Bank Leumi Le-Israel,* 303 St., House No. 1; *Israel Discount Bank Ltd.,* Casanova St.

Ramat Gan (pop. 109,400) (near Tel Aviv)

HOTEL: *Nordau,* 13 Nordau St., 14 rooms (8 sh.)

NIGHT CLUBS: The *Eden, Oasis,* and *Rendezvous* offer floor shows with a band for dancing.

SHOPPING: Bezalel jewelry and fine arts and craftswork at Reiskind, 36 Bialik St.; ladies' fashions at *Lola,* 48 Bialik St.

USEFUL ADDRESSES: Israel Discount Bank Ltd., 50 Herzl St.

Safed (pop. 13,000); (alt. 2,600 ft; Mt. Cana'an: 3,100 ft.)

HOTELS: ****Rimmon Inn,* ***Mines House,* Mt. Cana'an, 27 rooms (10 b., 17 sh.); ***Nof Hagalil,* Mt. Cana'an, 36 rooms (23 b., 13 sh.) (K); ***Ruckenstein,* Mt. Cana'an, 26 rooms (12 b., 14 sh.); ***Tel Aviv,* 32 rooms (12 b., 20 sh.); ***Rakefet,* center of town, 84 rooms (24 b., 60 sh.) (K), French and Italian cuisine, special natural foods, dining room; ***Ron,* 50 rooms (30 b., 20 sh.); **Central,* 37 Aleph St., 60 rooms (19 b., 41 sh.) (K); **Pisgah,* Mt. Cana'an, 50 rooms (16 b., 34 sh.) (K); *Yair,* 28 rooms (28 sh.) (K).

SHOPPING: Paintings, souvenirs, Bezalel art work from *Klein,* near Kiryat Hatzarayim, and *Venus,* 71 Jerusalem St.

USEFUL ADDRESSES: *Tourist Information Office,* Municipality Bldg.; *Bank Leumi Le-Israel,* 37 A-st. Safed is famous for its Artists' Colony as well as its medieval synagogues.

Shavei Zion-on-the-Sea (pop. ca. 300); (Haifa telephone exchange)

HOTELS: ***Dolphin House and Country Club,* 70 rooms (69 b., 1 sh.) (K, AR, S), excellent dining room, with nightclub, dancing; **Chava House,* 45 rooms (8 b., 29 sh.) (K, AR).

Tel Aviv (pop. 393,000)

HOTELS: *****Dan,* 99 Hayarkon St., 356 rooms (356 b.) (K, FA); *****Hilton,* 434 rooms (430 b.) (K, FA, S); *****Sheraton,* Nordau Blvd., 220 rooms (184 b., 36 sh.) (K, FA, S); ****Astor,* 105 Hayarkon, 68 rooms (53 b., 15 sh.) (K, FA); ****Basel,* 156 Hayarkon, 116 rooms (112 b., 4 sh.) (K, FA);

****Deborah, 63 rooms (63 b.) (K, FA); ****Ramat Aviv, Natanya Rd., 112 rooms (112 b.) (K, FA, S); ****Samuel, 100 rooms (100 b.) (K, FA); **Armon, 90a Hayarkon St., 18 rooms (16 b., 2 sh.) (FA); **Atlantic, 18 rooms (4 b., 12 sh.) (K, FA); **Eliat, 58 Hayarkon, 25 rooms (20 b., 5 sh.); **Excelsior, 88 Hayarkon, 24 rooms (2 b., 22 sh.) (FA); **Imperial, 66 Hayarkon, 24 rooms (10 b., 14 sh.) (AR); **Jacobson, 73 Gordon St., 19 rooms (14 sh.); **Narciss, 194 Hayarkon, 31 rooms (3 b., 21 sh.) (K, AR); **Kfar Hamacabia, 97 rooms (41 b., 56 sh.) (K, S); **Savoy, 5 Geulah St., 24 rooms (3 b., 19 sh.) (K, AR); **Yarden, 130 Ben Yehuda St., 44 rooms (13 b., 28 sh.) (AR); **Yarkon, 64 Hayarkon St., 39 rooms (5 b., 25 sh.) (AR); *Hanesiim (C1), 15 rooms (15 sh.) (K); *International (C1), 17 Allenby Rd., 8 rooms (AR); *Beach, 6 Allenby Rd., 15 rooms (4 sh.); *Europa, 42 Allenby Rd., 16 rooms (16 sh.); *Hagalil, 56 Allenby Rd., 9 rooms (AR); *Migdal David, 8 Allenby Rd., 20 rooms (11 sh.) (AR); *Monopol, 26 rooms (3 b., 22 sh.); *Nes Ziona, 10 Nes Ziona St., 13 rooms (6 b.); *Nordau, 14 rooms (8 sh.); *Palga, 2 Allenby Rd., 20 rooms (20 sh.) (K); *Sela, 52 Hayarkon St., 10 rooms (7 sh.); *Tamar, 8 Gnessin St., 7 rooms (7 sh.).

RESTAURANTS: Beit Sokolow, 4 Kaplan St., European cuisine (K), Casba, 32 Yermiahu St., French cuisine; Chin Chin, 4 Ben Yehuda St.; Dolphin, 15 Shalom Aleichem St., European; Fontainbleau, 193 Dizengoff St., European; Jeanette, Jaffa Port, famous fish spot; L'Auberge, Herzliya Rd., nr. Ramat Hasharon, French; Rishon Cellar, 11 Allenby Rd., European; Ron, 88 Herbert Samuel Esplanade, European; Tzli-Esh, 26 Allenby Rd., Oriental; Z.O.A. House, 1 Daniel Frisch St., European (K); Zuckerman, 39a Ben Yehuda St., vegetarian dishes.

NIGHT CLUBS: The Tel Aviv Theatre Club features floorshows highlighting Hebrew satire and wit, song and dance in an intimate and original setting; the Omar Khayyam, in a converted Arab dwelling in Jaffa, features Arab dishes and folk singing; the Cocktail Bar and the Hinga Bar have floor shows and an orchestra with a featured singer for dancing; the Sheraton-Tel Aviv, Dan, Ramat Aviv, Casino Bar, Dolphin Bar, Yarkon Bar, Ginat-Yam, Atom Bar and Bar 51 offer bands with a singer and dancing. Tel Aviv is also famous for its outdoor cafés where one may order anything from felafel through a full course meal to French or Italian pastries, while watching the crowds go by or participating in the lengthy and varied discussions that are an integral part of this café society.

MUSIC AND THEATRE: The Israel Philharmonic Orchestra performs regularly in the Fredric R. Mann Auditorium; the Israel National Opera makes Tel Aviv its headquarters; the world-famous Habimah, the Kameri (Chamber) Theatre and the Ohel (worker's theatre) offer both native Israel and foreign productions.

MUSEUMS AND LIBRARIES: Tel

The Western Wall of the Temple (Wailing Wall)

Aviv Museum, 16 Rothschild Blvd., contains works by old and new masters, has regular exhibitions and features Saturday night concerts; *Ha'aretz Museum,* opp. Ramat Aviv Hotel, houses an exhibit of glassware, pottery, coins; *Helena Rubinstein Pavilion of Contemporary Art,* Dizengoff St. next to Mann Auditorium; *Artists' Pavilion,* 9 Alharizi St., displays official exhibits of the Artists' Association; *Permanent Industrial Exhibition* of the Manufacturers' Association, 13 Montefiore St.; *Eliahu Golomb Haganna Museum,* 23 Rothschild Blvd., is devoted to the history of the Haganna, with exhibitions of arms, uniforms, photos, etc. *Beit Ahad Ha'am,* Ahad Ha'am St., is the home of the famous philosopher and contains his writings and library; *Tel Aviv-Jaffa Historical Museum,* 26 Bialik St., has exhibits relating to the history of the city; *Tel Aviv-Jaffa Museum of Antiquities,* 10 Mifratz St., displays archaeological finds from this ancient city; *Zoological Gardens,* 77 Keren Kayemet Blvd.

SHOPPING: *Gifts:* Beatus, 64 Allenby Rd.; Carmeli, 9 Ben Yehuda St.; Dan Souvenirs Ltd., Dan Hotel; Dolphin Shop, 106 Hayarkon St.; Freund Gifts, 41 Allenby Rd.; Film Star Ltd., 33 Allenby Rd.; Gal-Noy, 103 Dizengoff St.; Hamatanah, 54 Sheinkin St.; Henany, 73 Ben Yehuda St.; Jacobi Art & Gift Shop, 7 Allenby Rd.; Jacobson & Co., 54 Allenby Rd.; Lafayette, 1 Ben Yehuda St.; Maskit Israel Village Crafts, 40 Frishman St.; Menora Arts Ltd., 40 Allenby Rd.; Miki Gift Shop, 82 Allenby Rd.; Mizrahi's Workshop, 20 Nachlat Benyamin St.; S. Moradoff, 15 Ahad Ha'am St.; Nava, 111 Allenby Rd.; Omanut Hendel, 20 Ben Yehuda St.; Rachel, 45 Ben Yehuda St.; Radad, 80 Allenby Rd.; Reiskind, 36 Bialik St.; Riesel, 40 Allenby

The Dome of the Rock where Abraham bound Isaac for sacrifice to the Lord, and where tradition says Mohammed ascended to heaven

Rd.; Rivoli, 104 Allenby Rd.; A. Sarraf Kashani, 57 Allenby Rd.; Tarko Gifts, 26 Rambam St.; The Shop, Sharon Hotel; Tila, 13 Ben Yehuda St.; Topaz, 10 Malchei Israel Square; Topaz, 10 Dizengoff St.; Vardi, 156 Dizengoff St.; Wizo Shops,; 87 Allenby Rd. Yeroushalmi & Son, 42 Ben Yehuda St. *Art and antiques:* A. Boehm, 62 Ben Yehuda St.; W. Godny, 90 Ben Yehuda St.; Mikra Studio, 56 Allenby Rd.; Eliezer Rosenfeld, 147 Dizengoff St.; J. Stieglitz, 71 Allenby Rd. J. Tiroche, 110 Dizengoff St. *Toys:* Ortex, 122 Allenby Rd.; Shenker, 108 Allenby Rd. *Jewelry:* Fuhrer, 73 Allenby Rd.; Rais Bros., 37 Allenby Rd.; M. Werner Ltd., 84 Allenby Rd. *Leather goods:* Mayslitz, 94 Allenby Rd. *Shoes:* Atereth, 105 Dizengoff St.; Mandler, 101-103 Dizengoff St.; Phil-Shoes, 62 Al-

lenby Rd. *Flowers:* Iris Flower Shop, 68 Allenby Rd. *Books and music:* Harmony, 70 Ben Yehuda St.; Radio-Union, 116 Dizengoff St.; Scala, 41 Ben Yehuda St.; Sinai, 72 Allenby Rd.; Sommerfield Music Centre, 11 Ben Yehuda St. *Clothing:* Adam, 40 Allenby Rd.; Asco Ltd., 94 Allenby Rd.; Bifro, 27 Allenby Rd.; Englander Sisters, 66 Allenby Rd.; Fanchette Ltd., 126 Dizengoff St.; Feldman, 93 Allenby Rd.; Iwanir's, 31 Allenby Rd.; Mayer Bros., 69 Allenby Rd.; My Corner—Pinati, 67 Allenby Rd.; O.B.G., 43 Allenby Rd.; Salon Sarah, 62 Ben Yehuda St.; Taami, 15 Ben Yehuda St. *Children's wear:* Layeled, 50 Allenby Rd.; Alisa J. Gleicher, 118 Dizengoff St.; M. Singer, 11 Ben Yehuda St.; S. Birnhack, 98 Allenby Rd. 84 Allenby Rd.; Leophot, 12 Allenby Rd.; Photo Hadar, 38

Ahad Ha'am St.; Photo Karat, 83 Allenby Rd.

USEFUL ADDRESSES: *Tourist Information Office,* 7 Mendele St.; *Main Post Office and Philatelic Services,* 132 Allenby Rd.; *Telegraph Office,* 7 Mikve Israel St.; *Bank Leumi Le-Israel,* 19 Herzl St. (main office); *Israel Discount Bank Ltd.,* 27/29 Yehuda Halevy St. (main office); *Hadassah Overseas Club,* Hayarkon St.; *Mizrahi Tourist Club,* 14-16 Dov Hos St.; *Z.O.A. House,* 1 Daniel Frisch St. *Beauty parlors:* Alex Rubins, 2 Pinsker St.; Annetta, 18 Mapu St.; Rina, 111 Allenby Rd.

Tiberias (pop. 23,300);
(600 feet below sea level)

HOTELS: *****Galei Kinneret,* Hamerhatza'ot St., 68 rooms (62 b., 6 sh.) (K, FA); ****Ginton,* 63 rooms (60 b., 3 sh.) (K, FA); ****Guberman Grand,* 72 rooms (72 b.) (K, FA); ***Chen,* Ohel Ya'acov St., 70 rooms (50 b., 10 sh.) (FA, S); ***Daphne,* Ahuzat Kinneret, 40 rooms (20 b., 20 sh.) (K, FA); ***Peer,* Nazareth St., 56 rooms (9 b., 47 sh.) (FA); ***Ganei Hamat,* 80 rooms (80 sh.) (AR); **Sara,* 16 rooms (2 b., 9 sh.) (K, AR); **Eden,* 37 rooms (7 b., 30 sh.) (K, FA); **Menora,* 52 rooms (20 b., 11 sh.) (K, AR); **Ron,* 30 rooms (30 sh.); *Eshel,* 18 rooms (4 b., 10 sh.) (K); *Florida,* 11 rooms (1 b., 10 sh.) (K); *Ginossar,* 64 rooms (2 b., 62 sh.).

RESTAURANTS: The famous *Lakeside* (FA), excellent fish plus the glorious view over the Kinneret; the *Galei Kinneret,* fine kosher cuisine; the restaurant at *Kibbutz Ein Gev,* over the Sea of Galilee, fish specialties. Tiberias is a greatly frequented winter resort, famous for its hot springs. Its night spots, such as the *Arbel,*

An ancient synagogue in Capernaum

Picking apples

Lido and *Panorama*, each of which offers a featured singer with its dance band, are open only from November through March.

USEFUL ADDRESSES: *Government Tourist Information Office*, 8 Nazareth St., *Bank Leumi Le-Israel*, S. Hoofien St.; *Israel Discount Bank Ltd.*, Hagalil St.

Zikhron Yaakov (pop. 4,700)

HOTEL: **Dora Schwarz* (C1), 34 rooms (13 sh.); vegetarian cuisine. **Gafniel* (C1), 9 rooms (1 b., 8 sh.) (K).

KIBBUTZIM GUEST HOUSES

****Ayelet Hashahar, Upper Galilee, 80 rooms (40 b., 40 sh.) (K, AR, S); ****Nof Ginossar, Sea of Galilee, 64 rooms (10 b., 54 sh.) (K, FA); ***Beit Oren, Mt. Carmel, 85 rooms (6 b., 79 sh.) (S); ***Beit Yesha, Givat Brenner, 62 rooms (62 sh.) (AR); ***Hafetz Haim, Upper Galilee, 40 rooms (12 b., 28 sh.) (K, AR); ***Hanita, Western Galilee, 57 rooms (57 sh.) (S); ***Hagoshrim, Western Galilee, 40 rooms (38 sh.) (AR, S); ***Kfar Blum, Upper Galilee, 22 rooms (22 sh.) (K); ***Kfar Giladi, Upper Galilee, 65 rooms (9 b., 56 sh.) (K, S); ***Kiryat Anavim, 81 rooms (41 sh.); ***Lavi, Upper Galilee, 20 rooms (6 b., 14 sh.) (K); ****Ma'ale Hahamisha*, Judean Hills, 83 rooms (38 sh.) (S); ***Nir Etzion, Mt. Carmel, 87 rooms (72 sh.) (K); ***Shefayim, Sharon Plain, 86 rooms (53 sh.) (AR); **Gesher Haziv, Western Galilee, 40 rooms (2 b., 36 sh.) (AR).

YOUTH HOSTELS

Bar Giora Hostel (15 mi. southwest of Jerusalem), 170 beds; *Beit Ahim Hostel*, Ramat Hashofet (15 mi. south of Haifa), 130 beds; *Beit Benjamin Hostel,* Safed, 160 beds; *Beit Noam Hostel,* Sodom, 80 beds; *Biet Noam Hostel,* Mitspe Ramon (Negev), 160 beds; *Beit Sara Hostel,* Ein Gedi, 160 beds; *Beit Yatziv Hostel,* Beersheba, 250 beds; *Eilat Hostel, Eilat,* 168 beds; *Emek Hefer Hostel,* Kfar Vitkin (27 mi. north of Tel Aviv), 270 beds; *Givat Shamir Hostel,* Ramat Yohanan (10 mi. northeast of Haifa), 130 beds; *Hankin Hostel,* Gidona (27 mi. southeast of Haifa), 270 beds; *Israel Taiber Hostel,* Poria (5 mi. south of Tiberias), 100 beds; *Kiryat Tivon Hostel* (6 mi. east of Haifa), 70 beds; *Louise Waterman Wise Hostel,* Jerusalem, 120 beds; *Massada Hostel,* Massada (Dead Sea), 200 beds; *Meir Haezrahi Hostel,* Kiryat Anavim (7 mi. west of Jerusalem), 70 beds; *Tel Aviv Hostel,* 32 Bnei Dan St., 230 beds; *Tel Hai Hostel,* Tel Hai (37 mi. north of Tiberias), 200 beds. *Yad Layad Hostel,* Gesher Haziv (21 mi.

north of Haifa), 300 beds; *Yoram Hostel,* Karei Deshe, on the Sea of Galilee (6 mi. north of Tiberias), 120 beds.

These hostels offer dormitory accommodations with blankets (sheets may be rented for a small additional fee). Most serve meals, while all provide kitchen facilities. Rates are 28¢ for members and 45¢ for non-members in the age category up to 18; and 51¢ for members and 79¢ for non-members for those 18 and over. The Israel Youth Hostels' Association (P.O.B. 1075, Jerusalem), which operates all these hostels, is affiliated with the International Youth Hostels' Association.

CHRISTIAN HOSPICES

Jerusalem: *St. Andrew's Hospice,* Church of Scotland, near railway station (breakfast only); *St. Charles' Hospice,* Roman Catholic, German Colony; *Notre Dame de France,* Roman Catholic; *Sisters of the Rosary,* Roman Catho-

Ruins at Atlit

lic (French). East Jerusalem (Old City and suburbs): *Benedictine Sisters Monastery,* Mt. of Olives, Roman Catholic, French; *Casa Nova (Franciscans),* Old City; *Christ Church Hostel,* Jaffa Gate, Anglican Church, British; *Lutheran Hostel,* St. Mark's St.; *Pie Madri of Nigrizio,* Roman Catholic, Italian. Ein Kerem: *Soeurs de Notre Dame de Sion,* Roman Catholic. Nazareth: *Monastère des Prêtres du Sacré Coeur de Jésus de Betharram* (for pilgrims only), Carmelites-Roman Catholic (French); Mount Tabor: *Convento Francescano della Transfigurazione* (for pilgrims only), Franciscan-Roman Catholic, P.O.B. 16, Nazareth. Tiberias: *Ospizio Monte di Beatitudine,* Roman Catholic (Italian), Mt. of Beatitudes near Tiberias, P.O.B. 87; *Peniel-by-Galilee* (Dr. Hart's), Y.M.C.A., Protestant, on the shore of the Sea of Galilee, near Tiberias, P.O.B. 192 (no meals). Rates range from $3.99 to $4.96 per person per day for room and full board.

Elijah
Elisha